IRAN

IRAN

RICHARD N. FRYE

Harvard University

HENRY HOLT AND COMPANY New York

Contents

Iran and the Persian Gulf

CASPIAN
SEA
TABRIZ
AZERBAIJAN
TURKS
TURKOMANS
KURDS
MESHED
TEHRAN
KURDS
LURS
ISFAHAN
BAKHTIYARIS
AFGHANISTAN
ARABS
QASHQAIS
ZABUL
BRAHUIS
SHIRAZ
AFSHAR
TURKS
ZAHIDAN
KHAMSEH
TRIBES
AND
MINORITIES
BALUCHIS

See "Tribes and Minorities," Chapter 1, pp. 8-11.

The map of Iran (page vi) is reprinted by permission from *The Middle East Journal*.

IRAN

1

Land and People

IN THE second half of the twentieth century the Orient has become a bone of contention between the conflicting worlds of the West and the Soviet Union. But the issues here are far more complicated than great power rivalry, for nascent nationalisms and internal unrest in the countries of the East overshadow the issue of acceptance or rejection of Communism, and our relations with these countries must be based on an understanding of their internal problems, not solely on the black-white yardstick of their pro- or anti-Communist positions. Many of the problems are age-old and not to be solved overnight, nor by a universally applicable touchstone of American democracy. For much of what has been developed on American soil is a result of traditions and circumstances peculiar to our land and people. In transplanting our ideas and techniques to other countries we may find that they do not flourish or that they develop in directions other than those followed in America. This is especially true in Asia where there are ancient civilizations with cultural patterns different from the West European Christian tradition. And Asia itself is no unit; there are many peoples and cultures in that vast land mass. The countries vary in language, in religion, in level of industrialization, and in a host of other respects.

That is why one must study the background of a country like Iran to realize her peculiar problems and those features which distinguish this country from her neighbors. To put all of the peoples and countries of the Middle East into one category with little differentiation is a great error; each peo-

1

ple and nation must be examined separately in the light of geography, history, customs, and present conditions.

The oil of Iran has usurped the headlines concerning that little-known land, but Iran also has great strategic importance bordering the Soviet Union and acting as a land bridge between India and the Mediterranean states. She is a member of the free, non-Communist world—even though a weak member at present, bitterly embroiled with Great Britain over the oil question. Whether Iran remains free depends to a great extent on a solution of the oil problem, but in the long run it depends on Iran's ability to take her place in the modern world with all that this implies. The growing pains of "modernization" in Iran are legion, but they must be resolved if Iran is to survive, and it behooves us to understand, aid, and encourage the Persians in this difficult task of theirs. Before we can really help, we must understand; and for that we must study her past as well as the present.

THE LAND

Persia, or Iran as it is called by its inhabitants,[1] is a country almost as large as the United States east of the Mississippi River, a land of great variety in its physical features. High mountain ranges alternate with barren deserts or lush semi-tropical forests, all of which have tended to separate the people from each other rather than to bind them together in a geographical unity. And nature is extremely important in conditioning the lives of the people for they are closer to and more dependent on the whims of nature than we in the West. An exacting climate and an unwilling soil are not the least of the hardships which test the strength and patience of the Persian peasant and nomad.

The location of Iran, as a link between the Far East (with India) and the West during most of her history, and as an area of dispute between the Russians from the north and the

[1] In the West the form *Persia*, from the southern province now called Fars, is more common than *Iran*, from *Aryan*. In this book *Iran, Iranian* and *Persia, Persian* are used synonymously.

British from the south in more recent times, must be remembered in studying the past of the country and especially her role today in great power politics. Iran has also served as a highway for invading peoples from Central Asia, passing either to the east of the central deserts on the road to India, or to the west towards Iraq and Anatolia. Furthermore, the influence of Iran in political and economic, but especially in cultural, matters extended and still extends beyond her present political frontiers; geography helps to explain this.

The geographic unit of which present political Iran is the largest part comprises the plateau with mountains extending from the plains of the Punjab to the lowlands of Iraq. The plateau is bounded on the south by the Persian Gulf and the Indian Ocean, and on the north by the Caucasus Mountains and the plains of Central Asia. For our present purposes, however, we must exclude those areas of the plateau which are included in the boundaries of the Soviet Union, Afghanistan, or Pakistan.

The part of the plateau which is in Iran is by no means comparable to a billiard table; rather it is divided by many mountain ranges, narrow valleys, and wide deserts. It is roughly the shape of a triangle with the apex in the northeast, where Iran meets Turkey and the USSR, and the other two points where Iran touches Afghanistan and Russia and where she is bounded by Pakistan and the Indian Ocean. Outside the plateau, but within the political frontiers of Iran, are in the south the plain of Khuzistan, a continuation of the rich alluvial lowlands of Iraq, and in the north the Caspian littoral, which lies below sea level.

Two great mountain ranges divide the plateau from these plains; one of these, the Elburz, extends from the Caucasus south of the Caspian and into Afghanistan, with its highest peak, Mt. Demavand (18,600 ft.), visible to the east of Tehran. The other, the Zagros range, lies along Iran's western border and continues to the south along the Persian Gulf and Indian Ocean to Pakistan. Smaller mountains intrude into the interior of the country, and even in the central deserts mountains are never out of sight. These two deserts, the Dasht-i-

Kavir and the Dasht-i-Lut, are impressive in their desolation and loneliness. In them are salt craters reminiscent of the moon's surface seen through a telescope, and there is absolutely no animal or vegetable life.

In general, verdure and trees on the plateau are conspicuous by their absence, and only the agency of man, leading water to gardens and oases by irrigation, brings green to an otherwise naked landscape. Probably in the past there was more vegetation than there is today. For example, the first Moghul emperor of India mentions in his memoirs the verdure on the environs of the city of Kabul, Afghanistan, whereas today, after four hundred years, they are barren of vegetation. Nonetheless one wonders how much of the greenery then was due to the industry of the population, and whether much of the lack of it today is the result of neglect and depredations. There are traces of habitations and caravansarais in the deserts attesting to once populous areas where today there is no one, but this may be the result of shifts in population, and it is a question whether the population of pre-Mongol Iran, estimated by some at five or six times the present number of people, may not be an exaggeration.

In any case the mountains and valleys are the same, and now as then they divide the plateau into a number of parts. Excepting the two areas outside the plateau mentioned above, one may make ten divisions starting with Azerbaijan in the northwest, a geographical entity which from time to time has led a political existence apart from the rest of Iran. This is the only province of Iran where dry-farming is practiced. The heart of the country is the Tehran-Isfahan-Hamadan area, frequently the site of the capital, and the center of power in recent times. To the south is the important province of Fars, with its principal city of Shiraz, homeland of Iran's pre-Islamic dynasties. Further to the east is the province of Kirman, with its largest city of the same name, high in altitude, and its second city Bam. This area is isolated from the rest of Iran by deserts to the west between Kirman and Yezd, and to the east between Bam and Seistan. The latter is a flat plain watered by the Helmand River, which flows from the mountains of Afghanistan and rescues the land from the desert. Here one can lose sight of the mountains to the west and find himself in a rich farming area where Indian water buffaloes mingle with the sheep and goats of nomadic Baluchis. Farther to the south and east is the barren land of Baluchistan, at present divided between Iran and Pakistan.

In the northeast is the comparatively populous province of Khurasan (Khorasan), with its largest city, Meshed, the religious center of Iran. Here too are extensive poppy fields, producing the opium for which Iran is noted. Khurasan is separated from the rest of the country by the two great salt deserts, which, however, are not impassable, since oases and waterholes can be found along the caravan routes. The Turkoman steppes, though they may be regarded as the northern part of Khurasan, are better considered as a continuation of the steppes of Central Asia, extending south from the Soviet Union. Finally there is the wide Zagros mountain range in the west, inhabited by Kurds and Lurs, famous for their fierce, independent spirit. This division of Iran does not correspond to modern political divisions, but rather to historical and geographical factors.

In addition there is the oil province of Khuzistan at the head of the Persian Gulf and the caviar province of Gilan with Mazanderan province on the Caspian Sea. These areas are quite unlike the plateau in appearance and population. The plain of Khuzistan is cut by many rivers, including the only navigable river of Iran, the Karun. Whereas on the plateau the climate is continental, with cold winters and hot summers, in Khuzistan the winters are mild but the summers are characterized by the same unbearable heat as at Basra in Iraq. The present fame of Khuzistan rests on oil, for on the island of Abadan is the world's largest oil refinery, with pipes leading to the wells in nearby hills and mountains. While the oil industry has brought an unprecedented activity and development to this part of the country, it may, on the other hand, have contributed to a neglect of agriculture, for Khuzistan, famous in ancient times as a rich granary, is hardly that today.

The Caspian provinces are relatively the most densely

populated and, with humus soil, the richest agricultural lands in Iran. Here swiftly flowing rivers drop to the Caspian from high mountains, for the width of the coastal plain between sea and mountains is rarely more than a few miles. The abundant rainfall, in contrast to that of the plateau, and the warm climate produce areas of semi-tropical vegetation which the Persians call jungles. This area produces rice and silk, both of which are famous outside the borders of Iran. Gilan and Mazanderan have been for centuries exposed to raids and invasions from across the Caspian, the raiders including the Vikings in the tenth century and the Bolsheviks in 1920.

WATER

The cultivated soil, hardly more than one tenth of the total land area, is, over most of the plateau, a kind of loess becoming more and more sandy to the south and east. The great need in agriculture is water, the life blood of Iran, and irrigation must supply the major part of the country's needs. Since early times the Persians have maintained a remarkable system of irrigation with underground tunnels called *qanats* (or *ghanats*). These lead water from the mountains sometimes as much as thirty miles into the plains, underground to avoid loss by evaporation. Today, as for hundreds of years, they are dug and maintained by primitive methods, much labor, and a considerable outlay of capital. Deep wells are dug at intervals of about 150 feet, and then the bottoms of the wells are connected by a tunnel only large enough for a man with back bent to crawl through. Constant cleaning of mud and repair of cave-ins is necessary, though not an easy job, for the tunnels are sometimes as much as a hundred feet under the earth. Unfortunately most of the rivers on the plateau are seasonal streams, raging torrents for a short time in the spring and dry the rest of the year, and most of them empty into salt lakes or swamps. With the construction of permanent dams much water might be saved for agricultural purposes, and two such dams are under construction on the Helmand River in Seistan, while others are planned elsewhere in the country. Without large dams it is difficult to see how land reform and division of the land among the peasants will succeed, since water, not land, is important in Iran. And only the landlords at present have the necessary capital and ability to organize the peasants for labor on the *qanats*.

THE PEASANTS

As elsewhere in Asia, peasants are the great bulk of the Persian population. Estimates of the total population place it at about fifteen million with perhaps three quarters living in villages or on the land. Since World War II, however, there has been a great movement to the cities; Tehran, the capital, has now more than doubled its population from some half million before the war.

The life of the peasant has changed little in the past thousand years; it is still hard, little above the starvation level. He is constantly beset by disease—malaria, syphilis, tuberculosis—with diseases of malnutrition the most common. By nature conservative, he is difficult to persuade to change practices he inherited from his father and grandfather. The average peasant lives in a mud hut in a village which belongs to a landlord who may never visit the village if he owns scores just like it and affairs keep him in Tehran. There is usually a headman, or *kadkhuda*, in each village; in most cases he is the manager of the estates of the greatest landlord of the village or his appointee. It must be recognized that many landlords have treated their feudal domains paternally, taking care of the irrigation system and the peasants who are under them. Also, the amount of wealth many landlords derive from their villages is not always as great as one might suppose, since the margin above mere existence is small and there is little for the landlord to take.

Traditionally the produce of the land is divided into five parts, with one share each going to the persons who provide water, draft animals, labor, and seeds, while the landlord receives one fifth. If the peasant can provide oxen or seed he is in a better position than a neighbor who can only contribute his labor. In practice, however, the peasant is bound to the land, usually in eternal debt to the landlord. While this almost feudal system is accompanied by many abuses, it fosters also the paternalism and the kind of democracy where the landlord will sit on the floor to eat with his employees and peasants, providing for all. The problem of raising the standard of living of the peasant is of course basic to any plan for the progress of the country, and much more than a division of land is needed. Among other things there must be a long and painstaking education of the peasant on his responsibilities as well as his rights, while the landlord in time must be replaced by a trained and responsible farmer class.

TRIBES AND MINORITIES

The tribes are more important than their numbers (perhaps ten per cent of the total population) would indicate, for they are more disciplined and organized than settled folk—a necessity for the exacting life they lead. With sheep, goats, camels, horses, and sometimes cattle they move twice a year between summer and winter quarters, the former high in the mountains and the latter on the warmer plains. Reza Shah (1925-1941) tried unsuccessfully to break their organization and settle them on the land, but the result was not only a near disaster for the tribes but a disrupted economy between townsmen and their source of meat, hides, and the like. Many parts of the plateau are only suited for herdsmen, since they can be inhabited only in the summer; hence some form of pastoralism seems necessary.

Some tribesmen are settled, though still belonging to the tribe. More effective than Reza Shah's attempt to settle the tribes by force have been the opportunities to work in the oil fields or at Abadan, plus the conscription of youths for schools and for the army. Many tribal youths do not care to return to a strenuous nomadic existence after having seen the attractions of town life, and the tribes are having a more difficult time maintaining their strict organization.

The tribes have played an important role in the history of Iran, placing monarchs on the throne and supplying fine soldiers for the army. During the Constitution crisis in 1909 the Bakhtiyari tribe marched on Tehran to support the Constitutionalists against the Shah. They are a state within a state, for in tribal territory they set their own laws and so are frequently a thorn in the flesh of the central government at Tehran in its efforts to unify the country.

What are the principal tribes in Iran today? The most important are the Kurds, who number less than a million and who live in the highlands of the Zagros in western Iran. For the most part settled, they live under a strict tribal system with compatriots across the frontiers in Iraq and Turkey. The Kurdish language is written as well as spoken and there is an important nationalist movement among the Kurds, especially in Iraq. In 1945 a Kurdish republic was formed in Iran, but it was dissolved at the same time as the Azerbaijan republic in 1946. The majority of Kurds are Sunnite Muslims (Moslems), while the Persians and most other tribes are Shiites.

South of the Kurds, and speaking dialects closely related to Kurdish, are the Lurs and the Bakhtiyaris, who together may number half a million. The Bakhtiyaris spend the summer in the vicinity of Isfahan and the winter in Khuzistan. In the province of Fars the two principal tribes, both Turkish speaking, are the Qashqais (Ghashghais) and the confederation of the Khamseh (which has one sub-tribe of Arabs). At times these two tribes have been bitter rivals, and it is difficult to estimate their numbers.

In Khuzistan there are Arab tribes, although the oil industry has done much to settle many of the nomads. In Kirman province are Turkish-speaking Afshars, while further east are the Baluchis, the Afghans who speak Pushtu, and the Brahuis, who speak an archaic language said to be related to the Dravidian tongues of south India. They are few in number and (except for the Baluchis) not very important.

In Khurasan the once feared Turkomans have for the most part settled on the land, although there are still many nomads on the northern steppes. Here are also Kurds, settled by Shah 'Abbas in the early seventeenth century as part of his policy to mix the population and separate possibly trouble-some peoples.

The multitude of languages and dialects among the tribes is bewildering, but there are other settled minorities who even more complicate the composition of the population of Iran. Most important are the Azerbaijanis, who speak Turkish and who number somewhat less than two million. A well-known quip says the Azerbaijanis speak Turkish, write in Persian, and pray in Arabic. There is an Azerbaijan SSR in the Soviet Union just across the northern frontier.

We have been speaking of ethnic and linguistic minorities, but in the Muslim East the most significant distinctions among minorities are usually religious. Iran has more than her share of religious minorities. The largest group are the Armenians, numbering about 65,000 and mainly concentrated in the large cities, although there are Armenian villages near Isfahan and Tehran. Most of them belong to the Armenian national church, with headquarters in the Armenian SSR. With their own schools, newspapers, and clubs they form a group apart; still their influence in urban centers is con-siderable.

The Jews, with half the number of the Armenians, have not been attracted to Israel in great numbers, as have their co-religionists in other parts of the Middle East, since they enjoy comparative prosperity and freedom in the cities as merchants and professional men. They speak Persian though sometimes they write it in Hebrew characters.

The Christian Assyrians, numbering perhaps 20,000, live in the district of Lake Rezaiyeh (formerly Urmia). Some are also found in Tabriz and Tehran as artisans or business men. They are the remnants of the once important Nestorian Church, which in the Middle Ages extended its influence to China.

The pre-Islamic religion of Iran still claims 10,000 to 15,000 adherents in Yezd, Kirman and Tehran. The Zoro-astrians have not been fortunate in their relations with the

Muslims in the past, but since the time of Reza Shah they have been better regarded as representatives of Iran's ancient religion and culture. They are noted for their industriousness and good schools.

Finally, the Bahais must be mentioned, although they are not officially recognized as a religious minority. There are perhaps 100,000 of them, primarily among the educated classes in the towns. Their syncretistic, universal faith, which began in the last century, is regarded only as a Shiite heresy by many and they have not always been well treated by the Muslim majority.

The Jews and Zoroastrians are represented in the National Assembly by one member each, while the Assyrians and Armenians together have two representatives. The importance of the minorities lies to a great extent in their unity as organized groups; in general they have been free to practice their religion in peace.

GOVERNMENT

With such a diversity of peoples, tongues, and religions, what holds the nation together? In a number of respects Iran is similar to China. In both there is a long history of internal disunity and strong individualism, but solidarity in the face of the foreigner. In both there is the same reverence for the past and pride in Chinese or Persian culture. Indeed it is primarily the influence of Persian culture which has triumphed over the great physical and geographical obstacles to weld the various groups in Iran into one nation. Religion, of course, is of great importance, since the Persians are by it separated from their neighbors. But the central government is also an important factor in both countries, with the "mandate of heaven" in China and almost a "divine right of kings" in Iran. For until recently the institution of the Shahinshah of Iran was seemingly inviolate in its sanctity, and in the past the person of the monarch has been an important factor in maintaining the unity of the country.

Until the twentieth century Iran was a feudal state with

tribal chiefs and great landlords vying for favor with religious leaders at the court of the Shah. High-sounding titles were handed out to them by the sovereign to the tune of flattery and flowery praise of his rule and person. The only check on his autocracy was the advice of religious leaders or favorites. When Iran became a constitutional monarchy in 1907, the National Assembly was still overshadowed by a ruler who retained substantial powers of appointment, initiation of legislation, and other powers. Only in the reign of the present Shah Muhammad Reza Pahlevi has the prestige and the power of the parliament surpassed that of the monarch.

Since the parliament has usurped the place of the Shah as the symbol of authority and power, we should examine it in a little detail. The parliament is a manifestation of the aims of the people, who fought for a constitution almost fifty years ago, a constitution which is acclaimed by speeches and parades on its anniversary day every year. Although the original plans called for a parliament of two houses, the Senate, or upper house, did not come into existence until 1949, and it is the lower house or National Assembly (*Majlis* in Persian) which is far more important. According to the constitution the Majlis can have 162 deputies, elected by males over the age of 21, but present laws set the number at 136. The Senate has sixty members, half of whom are appointed by the Shah and half elected. Elections to the National Assembly are supposed to be held every two years, but they are not one-day affairs. Instead they last for months and are held at different times in the various cities and provinces, reputedly to reduce the possibility of concerted country-wide election riots. As in some European countries, deputies need not be residents of the districts which they represent in the Majlis.

The prime minister is elected by the Majlis and appointed by the Shah. Then his program, decided by him and his cabinet, must be approved by a majority of both Majlis and Senate. The prime minister and cabinet are responsible to the two chambers and must resign if there is a vote of no confidence. Bills voted by both houses become law when they are signed by the Shah.

In the days of the Reza Shah the Majlis was more or less a rubber stamp, and it has always been a group of wealthy landlords, religious leaders (who must be represented in the Majlis by law), and merchants. While it is hardly representative of the people as a whole, it has been responsive to public pressure. In the summer of 1952 the mob of Tehran discovered it could influence the members of parliament to do its will. Indeed, threats of assassination or retribution may have changed the votes of many deputies.

The Ministry of the Interior, through the Shah, appoints governors of provinces and, with the approval of the governors, the heads of districts and counties. So the local government is dependent on the central authority in Tehran, although in practice powerful landlords usually have their say in local affairs. Mayors of cities are likewise appointed by the Ministry of the Interior. This centralization has many drawbacks, especially in restricting the initiative and independence of local government officials who, if they are not fearful of their standing with Tehran, must at least be careful of their relations with local feudal lords. It has been a deliberate policy of the government in recent times to appoint officials to provinces far from their home province. In the elections of the winter and spring of 1952, governors and army, gendarmerie, and police officials were shifted from one province to another to avoid any complicity in influencing the elections. The policy of moving possibly rebellious tribes or groups of people from one part of the country to another is, of course, an ancient one in the history of Iran.

In cities and towns security is maintained by the police, also under the Ministry of the Interior. In villages and in isolated posts throughout the country, even in the deserts, peace is upheld by a well-trained gendarmerie force. Finally there are the army, navy, and air force under one ministry. Iran has a two year compulsory military service, but it is sometimes difficult to enforce in tribal territory.

The judicial system of the country, once entirely religious, has been secularized, and there are courts from the small district up to the Supreme Court. The organization of the courts has been based on the French system, with commercial, criminal, and civil codes. Although the judges are now graduates of the Faculty of Law of Tehran University, in villages and among tribes the *mullah* or Muslim "priest" is still the arbiter and magistrate for disputes.[2] There is constant surveillance to insure that no law goes contrary to the religion. Indeed the religious deputies in the Majlis may veto a law if they consider it contrary to the principles of the official religion of Shiite Islam.

RELIGION

Considerable space must be devoted to religion in Iran because religion for the Persians means much more than theology; it is traditionally their society, their law and culture, as well as their system of ethics and behavior. Islam is all inclusive, and in Iran there are features peculiary Persian which are added to the Islamic base. It is impossible here to elaborate on the principles of Islamic society, for they are many and not uncomplicated. Yet Muslims insist that their religion is simple, involving only five obligations: repetition of the phrase, "I believe there is no God but Allah, and Muhammad (Mohammed) is the prophet of God"; prayer five times a day; fasting from sunrise to sunset in the month of Ramazan; giving of alms; and the pilgrimage to Mecca.

The Quran (Koran), the holy word of God revealed to the prophet Muhammad, is more than an ethical guide and the road to salvation for a Muslim; it shows him how he should live and organize his state or society. More significant than personal ethics are the social ethics contained in it, though

[2] Formerly the *mullah* might be anyone versed in Islamic law and thereby qualified to administer it; today, however, the *mullah* has to study religion at an authorized school, after which he becomes a secular as well as religious leader in his community. The *mullahs* are very influential in the villages.

not always stated in unequivocal terms. Of course many Muslims, and especially the Sufis or mystics whom we shall discuss below, emphasize the personal rather than the social implications of the Quran, but they have always been in the minority. Consequently Islam has impressed Westerners with its monolithic character—it is an exacting faith whose forms are more binding on the believer than those of the Christian.

While the Muslim may pray and reflect in solitude, it is considered better to pray together with others of the faith, and the Friday prayers, on the Islamic day of rest, are impressive examples of seemingly disciplined rows of worshippers bending their backs in unison towards Mecca. The individualistic Persians, however, do not exhibit so frequently this massed show of unity in prayer which is more common among their neighbors, the Afghans and Arabs.

The official religion of Persia is the Shiite branch of Islam according to the Ja'fari ritual. To explain this we must turn to the early history of Islam, for the various Islamic sects differ among themselves more in their practices, and historically for political reasons, than in theology.

THE CALIPHATE

Since the prophet Muhammad founded a theocratic state, the question of a successor after his death in 632 A.D. was not only who could direct the Muslim armies and state, but who would be his spiritual successor, leader of the flock, and chief authority on religious matters. Muhammad had no sons, and only one of his daughters, Fatima, wife of 'Ali, had two sons, Hasan, and Husain (Hussein). There were some who thought 'Ali should succeed the prophet, but he was not chosen by the chiefs of the Muslim community. The first caliph, or successor of Muhammad, was Abu Bakr, and after his death two years later, the soldierly 'Umar (Omar) was selected. During his time Arab troops invaded Iran, an event which, among other considerations, has caused Persians to execrate his name. When he was assassinated in 642 A.D., 'Ali was neglected a third time and the aged 'Uthman (Othman) became caliph. The partisans of 'Ali continued to work for him, and when 'Uthman was murdered in 656 'Ali became caliph. But he had to contend against the family of 'Uthman, the 'Umayyads (Ommiads), whose members occupied important governorships in the now extensive empire of Islam. 'Ali was assassinated in 661, and the 'Umayyads, under the leadership of the governor of Syria, Mu'awiya (Mo'awiya), established a caliphate which lasted until 750.

This did not halt the activities of the Shiites or partisans of the family of 'Ali. When the son of Mu'awiya became caliph, Husain decided to oppose him, but he and his small band of faithful followers were surrounded and killed at Kerbela in Iraq, and this site has ever since been a great place of pilgrimage for Shiites.

Although the Shiite-Sunnite (those who accepted the 'Umayyads and came to be regarded as orthodox) split originated in what seems a political controversy, it is not easy to separate the religious differences from politics. Certainly with stabilization of the government attention turned more to spiritual matters, and the Shiites, denied political leadership in Islam, concerned themselves more with spiritual leadership. The office of caliph as political leader was distinguished from that of imam, or religious leader. (For the Sunnites the two were united in the person of the caliph; on the other hand there were many Shiites who never accepted the separation, deeming the *de facto* caliph a usurper.) For the Shiites the office of imam was hereditary in the family of 'Ali, and each imam named his son as successor until the twelfth imam in line from 'Ali disappeared without a successor when he was young. Thus arose the belief in the "Hidden Imam" or messiah who will appear again some day to lead his followers to salvation. Gradually a set of beliefs arose about the twelve imams: that they were infallible, sinless, and martyrs. A "martyrology" and "saint worship" consequently developed, and Shiites make pilgrimages not only to Mecca but also to Meshed, tomb of the eighth imam Reza, to Qumm, where his sister Fatima is buried, and of course to Kerbela and elsewhere. In addition there are many shrines of sons of imams (*imamzadeh*) in Iran which are visited by pious Shiites. It was Ja'far, the sixth imam, who worked out the rites and practices of Shiite law which are followed in Iran today. The Shiites emphasized the personalities of the successors of Muhammad as a kind of apostolic succession, which, of course, Sunnites could not accept.

Iran has been the Shiite country *par excellence* since the sixteenth century, but the faith of the masses contains many native Iranian (some pre-Islamic) beliefs and practices. The doctrine of the "Hidden Imam" resulted in a law system different from that which developed in the Sunnite realms.[3] In the latter law books were compiled which contained the reputed sayings of Muhammad (*Hadith* in Arabic) in clarification of ambiguous points in the Quran, or on subjects not mentioned in the Book. Since the Shiites did not accept these law books—instead relying on the interpretations of the Quran by the successive imams—they were in a sense less restricted than the Sunnites, especially after the twelfth imam. The Shiite religious leaders act for the "Hidden Imam," but only those who have attained a high standard of learning and the respect of the people can qualify for the role of interpreter of problems. Such a one is called a *mujta-hid*, and there are only a few in Iran at present. It is true that over the centuries the Shiites too have developed their traditions or law books, but the opinions in them can be changed by agreement.

There are many Shiite holidays, and the most impressive are the ten days of mourning for the death of Husain, culminating in public processions where believers beat themselves with chains and cut themselves with knives. A passion play depicting the slaughter of Husain and his followers is a popular feature of the mourning period.

Popular beliefs do not always seem in accord with Islam. The most important holiday is undoubtedly new year's day on March 21, the first day of spring, a purely Iranian holiday. There are many ceremonies and practices to celebrate the coming of the new year, some of which have to do with fire,

---

[3] As in Judaism, law is basic in Islam.

surely a survival from pre-Islamic times when the religion of Zoroaster, which placed great emphasis on fire, held sway in Iran. For the common folk the world is peopled with many unseen beings—fairies, *jinn*, and spirits both good and bad. And one must know the procedures and ritual to counter the influence of evil spirits. For example, one evil spirit is wont to attack travelers in the desert when they are sleeping and suck the blood out of a man through the soles of his feet. A story is told of a sure means of protection against this monster. Two men went to sleep in the desert feet to feet. The *jinn* approached and saw the head of one man. He quickly went to the other end to find the feet, but there he found another head. This so confused him that he went crazy and rushed away into the desert, one less such of his species. Divination by texts in certain books, by dreams, or by consulting the stars is quite popular, while belief in the evil eye sometimes causes trouble for blue-eyed foreigners.

DERVISHES AND SUFIS

Although the number and importance of wandering dervishes in Iran have declined considerably, one still sees these religious mendicants. They roughly correspond to the monks in medieval Christian society; they used to wander throughout the countryside with beggars' bowls and special costumes, writing charms on small pieces of paper to ward off sickness and the like. They were also great story tellers and givers of advice. Although Reza Shah forbade them they have now returned in reduced numbers.

The dervishes are the popular descendants of the Sufis or Muslim mystics who were deeply religious and who sought a direct, personal experience of God through means other than following the precepts of orthodox Islam. This mystical experience could be attained by various methods such as strict asceticism, prolonged thought, or music or dancing which would induce a trance—hence the "whirling dervishes." Various associations were formed which had their own routes and methods of attaining this oneness with God, and we have treatises of the mystics in Arabic and Persian. But in Iran it was primarily through poetry that the mystic expressed his feelings and his religion. Some of the finest examples of Persian poetry are mystical, expressing lofty sentiments in beautiful language. In a quatrain of expressive imagery perhaps the greatest Persian mystical poet, Jalal al-Din Rumi, says:[4]

> I sought a soul in the sea,
> And found a coral there;
> Beneath the foam for me
> An ocean was all laid bare.
>
> Into my heart's night
> Along a narrow way
> I groped; and lo! the light,
> An infinite land of day.

To this day such poetry is widely read in Iran and undoubtedly has now, as always, a great influence on the religious sentiments especially of the educated.

There are today important Sufi (from the Arabic word for wool, since the early mystics clothed themselves in woolen garments) or mystical organizations in Iran, but they are careful to dissociate themselves from the wandering dervishes, rather tracing their lineage from the philosophical mystics or the poets. In practice, however, they have become organizations like the Masons or the Knights of Columbus. Some fifty odd years ago a Sufi order was founded in Tehran by a confident of Nasr al-Din Shah, one Safi 'Ali Shah, which is at present flourishing in the capital. Another important order is the Nimat Allah, with its center at Mahan, a small town near Kirman, while a third, the Salih 'Ali Shah order, has its headquarters in Khurasan. The Sufi orders are quite liberal and they are trying to meet the religious needs of many of the Muslims, especially the young, who are faced with the impact of the West as a challenge to Islam. The Sufi orders are better able to accommodate Western influences

[4] Quoted by A. J. Arberry, *Sufism* (London, 1950), 117.

with Islam—at least their form of Islam—than is the formal Shiite state religion, for the Sufis place religion on an individual rather than a social basis, which allows them greater ease in coping with the problems of Westernization.

What is the position of religion in the lives of the people today? It must be remembered that until recently education was in the hands of the *mullahs,* who taught reading, writing, and the Quran to the children. All law was also administered by the religious leaders, and their influence in governmental affairs was considerable. This has now changed, and neither justice nor education is controlled by the *mullahs;* nonetheless their influence is still very much felt. The question of secularism and the impact of the West on the Shiite faith of Iran would require volumes; but suffice it to say that the Persians have not succumbed to the onslaught of the West but have taken and adapted much, with their genius for adaptation, and have if anything exalted their own culture even more.

CULTURE

The continuity of Persian culture is remarkable; the Persians have always been conscious of and have kept alive their national traditions in the face of foreign invasion and conquest. History for the Arabs more or less begins with Muhammad, since Islam superseded all that came before it; but this was not true in Iran, where native customs, language, literature, and the arts were too deeply imbedded in the people to be uprooted and replaced. As has been noted above, Persia is quite similar to China in these respects. There has always been a vague feeling of superiority and at the same time hospitality towards foreigners. In the past Iran was a center of civilization and culture from which influences radiated to the nomads of the northern steppes, to India, and towards the Mediterranean in the west. In recent times perhaps the Persians have developed a kind of insularity on their mountainous plateau, but the empire of the lion and sun was one of the centers of civilization in world history, and this should not be forgotten.

The central fact of this culture is not so much that Persians of all classes know their history, for they do not; nor that they hearken back to Iran's glorious past, though this they do. It is rather this somewhat intangible feeling among the people that Persian culture—traditions, outlook on life, and the like—will always survive political domination and the onslaught of new ideologies, and that it is a privilege to partake of this culture. That is why the Azerbaijanis or Baluchis and other "minorities" in Iran are Iranians and not of Turkish or other allegiances.

Although there is no one feature which stands above others as characteristic of Iranian culture, as for example the tradition of law and justice among the Anglo-Saxons, still perhaps stronger than any other trait is the love and appreciation for art and literature which is the legacy of Persia alive in the people today. This is seen first in the language and then in the arts.

LANGUAGE

The modern Persian language is a member of the Indo-European family of languages and, together with most of the tongues of India, belongs to the Aryan or Indo-Iranian branch of the family. This branch has one of the oldest literatures and has been less changed from the reconstructed mother Indo-European language than other members of the family. The two most ancient forms of Iranian are the Old Persian language of the cuneiform inscriptions of the Achaemenids, and Avestan, which is the language of the sacred book of the Zoroastrians. From this ancient stage there is a direct continuity to the Middle Iranian languages of the Parthians and Sassanians. Finally we have the modern period of Persian, with remarkably little change in the language, since prose and poetry of the eleventh century A.D. can be understood with ease by any literate Persian today.

The Arabic words which entered the language after the

seventh century A.D. provide the main distinction between modern and middle Persian. While modern Persian is written in the Arabic script, it has been modified so that Persian forms of writing are more beautiful than the Arabic. Persian grammar is simple, having no genders, articles, or real declensions, and the verb conjugations are almost always regular. It is a harmonious language—dubbed the Italian of the Orient—and admirably suited for poetry.

LITERATURE

George Washington and Abraham Lincoln are probably the best known and most esteemed Americans in this country; Sa'di and Hafiz are certainly the best known Persians in Iran. Illiterate shepherds, merchants, and villagers know by heart verses of Hafiz, the most beloved poet of Iran, while professors, journalists, and politicians are poets in their own right. Judges will quote a verse to admonish culprits brought into court. In the Middle Ages books on mathematics, astronomy, religion, and history were written in poetry. In spite of the wide range of poetry a poet had to obey rigid rules; "the domination of Classicism in French literature was moderate compared with the dictatorship of correct vocabulary and composition in Persia."[5]

Many reasons may be found for the importance of poetry in Persian literature other than an innate gift for and love of it. The Persians have ever been fond of moral precepts and philosophizing, and poetry provided an excellent vehicle for their enunciation. Furthermore poetry is much easier to retain in the memory, and as such was excellent for teaching the young. Poetry was the best way of making abstract concepts concrete and of making them comprehensible to the masses. It was also the means by which mystics and freethinkers could safely express their ideas in allegorical language. We find some surprising stanzas from Muslim Persians who were great poets, such as 'Attar (ca. 1150-1230 A.D.):

[5] A. J. Arberry in *Life and Letters and the London Mercury*, Vol. 63 (1949), No. 148, 233.

> We are the Magians of old,
> Islam is not the faith we hold;
> In irreligion is our fame,
> And we have made our creed a shame.[6]

And from Hafiz:

> If Muhammadanism be that which Hafiz holds,
> Alas if there should be a tomorrow after today.[7]

On being accused of heresy, Hafiz attributed this verse to a Christian whom he heard in passing a wine shop.

One will immediately ask how it is possible for the Persians as Muslims to permit the drinking of wine, praised not only by Omar Khayyam but by many other poets, and the representation of the human form in painting—a feature of Persian miniatures—both of which are forbidden by their religion. One answer is that the individualistic Persians have always stressed personal beliefs rather than outward practices of religion. They have been notably tolerant of this individualistic trait, and poetry, of course, demands this freedom.

Although the poets of Iran are legion, four stand out as masters in their respective forms of poetry. The first is Firdausi, who lived at the court of the Turkish Sultan Mahmud of Ghazna, in present Afghanistan, at the beginning of the eleventh century. His most important work is the *Shah Name,* "Book of Kings," an epic of the heroic legends of pre-Islamic Iran in about 50,000 distichs. He tells the history of Iran down to the Arab conquest in somewhat monotonous verses, but it is the subject matter rather than the style which endears him to his countrymen, for here are found the stories of all the early Iranian heroes, favorite subject matter of story tellers. Wrestlers today recite verses from the *Shah Name* before they grapple, and Firdausi's verses are used for cornerstones, mottos, and the like.

Jalal al-Din, known as Rumi because he lived at Konya in

---

6 A. J. Arberry, *Immortal Rose* (London, 1948), 36.
7 E. G. Browne, *A Literary History of Persia,* Vol. III (Cambridge, 1928), 281.

Anatolia, has been mentioned earlier. He died in 1273 after founding the Mevlevi or "whirling" order of dervishes and after writing, among other things, his famous *Masnavi,* a long didactic poem on the entire scope of mysticism in Islam up to his day. He opens his work using "the imagery of the reed-pipe to portray the mystic's desolate cry to God."[8]

> Hearken to this Reed forlorn,
> Breathing, ever since 'twas torn
> From its rushy bed, a strain
> Of impassioned love and pain.
>
> The secret of my song, though near,
> None can see and none can hear.
> Oh, for a friend to know the sign
> And mingle all his soul with mine!
>
> 'Tis the flame of Love that fired me,
> 'Tis the wine of Love inspired me.
> Wouldst thou learn how lovers bleed,
> Hearken, hearken to the Reed!

Sa'di of Shiraz (died 1291 A.D.) is a great moralist who presents stories based on his wide experience in his most famous work, the *Gulistan* or "Rose Garden," written when he was an old man. His teaching is simple but not always in accord with our standards of ethics, for he says at the end of his first story in the *Gulistan,* "A lie which mingles good will is better than a truth which stirs up mischief."[9] The kind of aphorisms in which his works abound are illustrated by the following: A king in counsel to his sons said the words so familiar to every Persian—

> For though ten dervishes upon one blanket
>   can lie down,
> Within one clime two kings can never wear
>   in peace the crown.

[8] A. J. Arberry, *Sufism, op. cit.,* 111.
[9] R. Levy, *Persian Literature* (London, 1923), 62.

Again:

> A casual word, pronounced in merest joke,
> To meditation will the wise provoke;
> A scroll of wisdom to the fool recite,
> He'll take it as a joke for his delight.[10]

The greatest and most popular lyric poet is Hafiz, who died in Shiraz about 1389. In his poetry he is a severe critic of pedantry and hypocrisy and the lack of sincerity among his contemporaries. Like Omar Khayyam he sings the praises of wine and lovers, which, however, must be interpreted by reference to their mystical significance, which was well developed by Hafiz's time. His *divan,* or collection of poems, is used by Persians as a book of augury. The book will be opened with eyes closed, and then the line or verse upon which the eye alights is taken to provide a guide to future action. One of his verses says:[11]

> When thou passest by our tomb, seek a blessing,
>   for it shall become a place of pilgrimage for
>   the libertines of all the world.

A story is told that the *mullahs* did not wish to bury Hafiz in a Muslim cemetery because of suspected heresy, but an augury was taken from his *divan* which decided the question:

> Withhold not thy footsteps from the bier of Hafiz,
> For, though he is immersed in sin, he will go to Paradise.

It would be a mistake, however, to assume that all of Persian literature is poetry. After the Muslim conquest of Iran, the Arabic language became the vehicle of science and learning all over the Islamic world, so that Persians wrote in Arabic. Later, when Persian came into its own as a literary language, prose works on history, medicine, astronomy, and others were composed in Persian. Indeed the productions in Persian during the Middle Ages entitle it to consideration as one of the great literary languages of the world.

---

[10] A. J. Arberry, *Kings and Beggars* (London, 1945), 86.
[11] Browne, *op. cit.,* 311.

THE ARTS

Persian art, like its poetry, has been decried for its excessive formalism and adherence to tradition. One may seek in vain for hidden purposes or a message in the mind of the artist when one studies the intricate designs of an object and the astonishing skill of the Persian craftsman, for design and decoration are the chief features of Persian art throughout the centuries. It may be objected that this limited the forms of art. While this objection may be valid in comparing Persian art with that of the Occident, yet no one can deny that Iran was ever a treasure house of the arts, a source from which her neighbors drew in abundance. Of course the Persians too borrowed much from other peoples, but they adapted what they received to the special requirements of their genius. For example, the Arabic script was developed and used for decorative purposes by the Iranians to a far greater extent than by the Arabs themselves.

What have been the art forms in which the Persians have excelled? In the minds of most of us carpets and miniature paintings are the most outstanding contributions of Iran to the arts. What can one say of the beautiful hand-woven rugs which have found places in many American homes? In spite of the synthetic analine dyes and the standardization of patterns, and those not the finest, the rugs of Kirman are still in quality probably the best now made. Today there is an average of 10,000 rugs exported yearly from Kirman, while from other weaving centers such as Meshed, Kashan, and Yezd come more, swelling the total number. It takes many months to weave a rug, and the weavers are often small girls seven or eight years of age. The various weaving centers have their own distinctive patterns, weaves, and also wool; the environs of Kirman are justly famous for the fine quality of wool on their sheep. The Persian's dislike of a bare surface without design makes their medallion or flower-filled carpets seem too ornate for many Westerners, but severe lines and empty spaces on rugs are incomprehensible to a Persian.

The same is true of miniature paintings, where empty stretches of sky, landscape, or water are displeasing to the artist. Human and animal figures, and decoration, usurp the scene in the miniatures even though such representation runs counter to the precepts of the Islamic religion. The tradition of painting is old in Iran. In late Islamic times schools of painting developed, and some of the extant miniatures from the fifteenth and sixteenth centuries are exquisite examples of the Persian artistic genius.

In architecture too Iran has produced masterpieces and has given distinctive forms to the world. The mosques of Isfahan are justly world-famous, and the profuse use of tile gives them a character unique in the Islamic world. The squinch, enabling a round dome to be placed on a square building, the *aiwan,* or huge arch and niche facing the central courtyard as transition stage from the interior, and the garden pavilion of tall, slender columns supporting a flat roof, are probably all Persian contributions to architecture. Persian gardens too have provided European and American planners with ideas.

Nor should one overlook the minor arts—pottery, bookbinding, metal work, wood inlay, and others—for Persians have always had a reputation for such work. Medieval Persian ceramics are second to none in form, coloring, and glaze, while carved wooden spoons and the inlaid wooden boxes of Fars province are still the delight of tourists as well as the local populace.

Music, of course, is in another category, but Iran seems to have been the major source for what today can be called "Near Eastern" music. It is difficult for a Westerner to learn to appreciate, and it is by no means uncomplicated as some may think.

CONCLUSIONS

The burden of the past rests heavily on the Persian of today. Although power and empire are gone, the Persians, like the French, can take comfort in the strength of their culture. Indeed, Iran has often been compared with France—

there is the same love of the arts, individualism, and regard for the emotions among both peoples—but the analogy can be exaggerated. There is a great resilience among the Persians; through centuries of domination by foreigners they have withstood the influences of conquest, in the end conquering their conquerors. In Iran, Turkish rulers have become more Persian than their subjects, and in spite of the great diversity of peoples, the culture of Iran has helped to form a nation.

While the Persian is proud of his past, he is not a chauvinist, and like the Arab he is conscious of affinity with his compatriots more because of language and culture than because of state or nation. The inhabitants of Iran are great non-conformists and exhibit a great diversity of opinion, but their individualism is both a praiseworthy trait and a handicap, especially in affairs where collective action is a necessity. This has been manifest in history when the enemy has profited from a policy of *divide et impera*. Certainly the history of British-Russian competition in Iran is replete with examples of competing partisan groups.

The uncommon ability to laugh at oneself is rather widespread among Persians, and, while they are filled with moral sentiments voiced in proverbs, admonitions, and thoughts of the world to come, they have a sense of humor which is more characteristic of them than of their more stolid neighbors, the Turks or Afghans. The story is told of a missionary who was leaving Iran after 30 years, having made only two converts to Christianity. With a feeling of unfulfilled mission, he told this to a distinguished Persian friend, who at once congratulated the astonished missionary on his success. "After all," he said, somewhat facetiously, "Muhammad has been trying for hundreds of years and has not yet converted a single Persian."

2

Empires of the Past

IT HAS BEEN said that the Oriental's concept of time is different from that of the Westerner. For the latter, time may be considered as relative to man and his actions; for the former, time is absolute, independent of man, who in his insignificance can only accept what the changes of fortune may bring. Whatever it may be, there is among Orientals an "otherness" which the admirer may call serenity, or the critic, fatalism. Yet if this attitude of mind is taken as a general characteristic of the Orientals, there is still a great diversity of its manifestations among the various peoples of the East. In India this attitude, along with many other factors, seems to have contributed to a lack of interest in history and the recording of events. Whatever may be said of the Persian's concept of time, however, he certainly did not neglect his history. The amount of historical literature written by Persians in the first millennium after the death of Muhammad is only rivaled by the Chinese histories.

There were many kinds of history books written by Persians in the Middle Ages, either in Arabic or Persian, including detailed chronicles year by year, mostly of political and military events. Other works include not a few city chronicles, describing the environs, famous people born or buried there, and outstanding events in the city's past. One must also include collections of biographies, historical geographies, and books of travel containing much of antiquarian interest. Most of the source material of the history of Iran has not been touched. If there is any dominant theme common to all of these books, however, it is the Islamic religion which set the standards of interest for both author and reader. And so it is that if one would understand the Orient, he must not only realize the importance of religion but be sympathetic to it.

Like the seasons and the passage of night to day in the East, the stages of Iran's history are clearly and sharply defined. If one would speak of the great changes in the course of her history, the most important division would be the Arab conquest in the seventh century A.D., making a convenient dichotomy into pre-Islamic and Islamic times. Nothing has been quite comparable to the impact which Islam made on Iran, not even the great influence of the West in recent times. For Islam molded the very bases of everyday life, not to mention the culture and thought, of the Persians from that time to the present. Just as we are part of the West European Christian tradition, so the Persians belong to the Near Eastern Islamic tradition and must be considered in relation to the wider culture of which they are a part. An examination of the structure and significance of that wider culture is beyond the scope of this book, but reference to it here and there is both necessary and inevitable even while concentrating on the features which distinguish Iran from her colleagues within the same general culture.

How does the "invasion" of the West fit into the pattern of Iran's history? One may conveniently illustrate this in a simple diagram showing the successive exterior forces or civilizations which have altered or greatly influenced the development of the Persians to the present. In this scheme the relative importance of the events can be indicated by asterisks—the Islamic conquest by four, those of lesser importance by three, and so on. The criterion for judging the significance of the various stages of her history is the part played in forming the Iran of today, although some of them may seem as distant from the Iran of 1953 as the ancient Greek civilization is from Broadway. The scheme I propose is the following:

    **Achaemenid first "world state," 6th-4th centuries B.C.
    ***Conquest of Alexander the Great and subsequent Hellenism, 331-129 B.C.

*Parthian-Roman and Sassanian-Byzantine rivalry: "East versus West," 130 B.C.-641 A.D.
****Arab conquest, 7th century A.D.
**Turkish-Mongol invasions, 10th-13th centuries.
*Safavid-Ottoman conflict, 16th-18th centuries.
***Impact of the West, 19th-20th centuries.

The significance of several of these stages is at once apparent; that of others does not become clear so quickly. The Achaemenids gave Iran her first great empire, the "one world" of antiquity, and set the pattern of state and government organization for dynasties in later epochs. Throughout history the Persians have looked back with pride to the golden age of the Achaemenids, much as Greeks today revere the Athens of Pericles, and, on a much reduced scale, as the French honor Napoleon.

Hellenism was fully as great an influence in the Near East in its time as the impact of the West is now. New ideas of science, philosophy, religion, architecture and others left their mark in Iran. One need only see the Greek statuettes, coins, and ruins of buildings uncovered every year in Iran or Afghanistan to realize that Greek culture not only gave ideas to the intelligentsia but penetrated to the very materia of ordinary life in Parthian and Sassanian times.

The rivalry of Parthians with Romans and Sassanians with Byzantines resulted in a division of the world between East and West, with Iran turning away from the Mediterranean towards Central Asia and India. This is the period during which the center of gravity of Iranian power and civilization shifts from the Southwest (Fars and Khuzistan) to the northeast (Khurasan), a process which was hastened by the Arab conquest. Hitherto the eastern part of Iran had played an insignificant role in history, but trade contacts with the Far East and India gave Iran a new importance as an intermediary between the distant Orient and Europe.

The Arab or Islamic conquest caused far-reaching changes in Iran, too many to discuss here, but above all it brought Iran into a great community extending from the Pyrenees Mountains to the Indus River. Iran became part of the Islamic world and henceforth the demands and prohibitions of an aggressive religion and a dynamic way of life were to dominate, yet eventually fuse with, old Iranian customs, philosophy, and concepts of art and architecture.

The Turkish-Mongol invasions changed the ethnic face of Iran so that today the majority of people in Azerbaijan speak Turkish, while Turkish-speaking tribesmen are scattered throughout the country. And again Iran was drawn towards the Far East and Central Asia, for she submitted to Mongol rule for over a century, a domination which the Arab lands for the most part escaped. Persians blame the destructive and wanton Mongol invasion for their decline and cite it as the prime reason why they fell behind while Europe developed apace.

The Safavid-Ottoman intermittent conflict from 1514 to about 1720 shut off Iran from Europe even though a few merchants and travelers did manage to reach the domains of the Shah. It was during this period that Iran produced the wonderful mosques, carpets, miniatures, and other works of art which are the delight of all the world. But this period is regarded by Persians as a feeble and ultimately unsuccessful attempt to recover from the ravages of foreign conquest.

Finally we come to the impact of the West, which may prove to be as important in the future as Islam was in the past. Perhaps the greatest symbols of Westernization in Iran are the constitution and the parliament wrested from an autocratic ruler in 1906. Parliament has now replaced the Shah as the center of power and authority, and perhaps even of respect. Before examining the role of the West, however, we must study the history of Iran before the 19th century, when European powers became involved in her affairs. It is not enough to speak of the recent past, for the whole story must be told; and for the Persians, to all intents and purposes, the story begins with the Achaemenids.

THE ACHAEMENIDS

Although Iran has more than her share of prehistoric mounds and sites, far too little archaeological work has been done to permit a reconstruction of her history before the advent of the Achaemenids. Much of the archaeological activity has been carried on at Susa and elsewhere in Khuzistan, which, as noted above, geographically is an extension of the Mesopotamian lowlands rather than part of the plateau. Since one finds Indo-European names in the cuneiform tablets of the Kassite period in Mesopotamia, one may surmise that there were Indo-European–speaking peoples in Iran as early as 2000 B.C. What the original inhabitants were like one can only guess. Some scholars have related them to the Sumerians, who were the first people to develop a high culture in southern Mesopotamia and who spoke a language unrelated to any other at present known. Others propose that the early people on the Iranian plateau were part of a large family, the survivors of which are the Brahuis in Seistan and Baluchistan.

About 1000 B.C. other Indo-European speakers came into Iran from Central Asia or from South Russia by way of the Caucasus Mountains. Whether these people were predominantly Nordic, Alpine or Mediterranean in race we cannot tell without considerably more anthropological and archaeological research, if ever. But they spread over Iran, speaking Iranian tongues which have developed into such modern languages as Persian, Kurdish, Baluchi, and Pushtu, as well as dialects of Persian such as Gilaki, Sivandi, and Khuri, designated after the localities where they are spoken. These people belonged to the eastern branch of the Indo-European speakers, the Aryans, or Indo-Iranians as they are sometimes called. One group went into India while the other remained in Iran.

The customs and religion of the early Iranians may be reconstructed from scanty notices of them in Assyrian cuneiform records, from later Greek historians, from the Avesta, and by analogy with the customs of present-day Iranian tribes. They probably owed their conquest of the Iranian plateau to an extensive use of cavalry and better weapons. One may regard the Turkish invasions of the eleventh to fourteenth centuries A.D. as comparable to this earlier conquest. Until the invention of firearms, nomads had an advantage over settled folk, and we may suppose that superior discipline and organization in the tribe plus mobility enabled the Iranians to conquer the settled people and make a home for themselves. The leading clan of the tribe which moved south into Persia, the present province of Fars, was the Achaemenid, so named after an eponymous chief at the time of the migration, which took place in the ninth century B.C.

In the north were other Iranians, known to their neighbors and to the Greeks as Medes. It seems that they were the first Iranians to develop a state with king and organized government. The little we know about the Medes comes from Assyrian sources and from Herodotus, who, incidentally, also tells us the one Median word which has survived, the word for "dog," *spaka*. At first the Medes suffered from Assyrian armies, who in the eighth century B.C. were the scourge of the entire Near East, and for many years the Medes were subject to the formidable Assyrian power to the west. The events which led to the overthrow of Assyrian overlordship and the establishment of a Median empire are shrouded in obscurity, but one name stands out as the founder of Median power, the king called Phraortes by Herodotus. He was probably the ruler who united the Medes and secured the submission of the Persians to the south about 670 B.C. Further Median expansion, however, was checked by the death of Phraortes and by a revival of strength of the Assyrians under Ashurbanipal. For some years the Medes also had to contend with nomadic Scythians, who invaded their land from the north, but Cyaxares, son of Phraortes, was able to capture Nineveh, capital of Assyria, with the aid of the Babylonians in 612 B.C. and to extend the boundaries of the Median empire far into Anatolia.

Although there have been no archaeological excavations, we can safely assume that the modern city of Hamadan rests on top of Ecbatana, the ancient capital of the Medes. Here was the treasury, according to a Greek author of the 1st century B.C.,[1] and extensive archives, both probably copied from Assyrian models. Much of the later Achaemenid state

[1] Isidore of Charax, *Parthian Stations*, I, 6.

organization was adopted from the Medes, and the Persian monarchs probably maintained their treasury and archives at Ecbatana even though their capital was at Susa or Persepolis. We can only surmise this, since no Achaemenid imperial records have been unearthed at the last two sites, while gold tablets with Old Persian cuneiform inscriptions have been found near or at Hamadan. Furthermore, in the book of Ezra VI, 2, it is reported that Darius found a decree of Cyrus at Ecbatana permitting the temple at Jerusalem to be rebuilt—this implying that the Persian as well as the former Median archives were located in Ecbatana.

While the Medes had been consolidating their power in the north, their vassals, the Persians in the south, were not idle. The Persian tribes had come from the north to the mountain area northeast of Khuzistan, to which they gave the name Parsumash. Here they built their first capital with a royal citadel rising over an artificial platform extending from a hill onto the plain at a place today called Masjid-i-Sulaiman (the temple of Solomon).[2] They may have brought this concept of a platform with them from their first northern home. Later the Achaemenids moved into Parsa, where a similar platform was erected at Pasargadae, their second capital. It was Cyrus II, called the Great, who built in Pasargadae some of the buildings the foundations of which have been cleared recently by Persian archaeologists. Cyrus revolted against his Median overlord Astyages about 553 B.C. and was completely successful capturing Ecbatana and inheriting the empire which the Medes had created. He was even more successful in uniting the Persians and Medes so that their names have been linked together throughout history, notably in the Old Testament and in Greek histories.

The armies of the Persians and Medes soon conquered Babylon and the rest of the "Fertile Crescent"—Syria and Palestine. Under Cambyses, son and successor of Cyrus, Egypt was added to the empire, the largest which had hitherto existed. It is a tribute to its stability that it survived the accidental death of Cambyses and subsequent revolts. Darius,

[2] Cf. R. Ghirshman, "Masjid-i-Solaiman," *Syria* (1950), 205 ff.

a noble from a collateral line of the Achaemenids, was able to put down the dozen or more revolts and became ruler of a domain even larger than that of Cambyses. He vanquished the opposition in 522 B.C., a year after Cambyses' death.

Darius was the real architect of the Achaemenid empire. He began the great platform and buildings at Persepolis, where the ruins still inspire the wonder of tourists. He also caused the mountain of Behistun near Kirmanshah to be carved with parallel inscriptions in three languages, Elamite, Akkadian, and Old Persian, the last of which had been committed to writing only a short time before. It was this Old Persian inscription which provided the key for understanding all of the languages written in cuneiform, and the story of its decipherment in the early nineteenth century, by Sir Henry Rawlinson among others, is as fascinating a tale of cryptanalysis as ever came out of the late world wars. To preserve the rock carving and inscriptions from vandals, Darius had the stone-carved steps leading up to it cut away and the surface smoothed so that full access to it had to wait the block and tackle of Western scholars. In the inscription, after telling of the various rebels he defeated and killed, he says, "This is what I did; by the favor of Ahuramazda, in one and the same year I did [it]. Thou who shalt hereafter read this inscription, let that which has been done by me convince thee; do not thou consider it false."[3] Then he admonishes future kings to beware of the Lie and to punish those who do evil.

The governmental organization which the Achaemenids instituted was remarkably flexible and a model for later states. Ruling over diverse peoples and religions the Achaemenids were not only tolerant in religious matters, but actually exerted themselves to show honor to the various religions of the empire. It was Cyrus was permitted the Jews to return to Palestine from captivity in Babylon and rebuild their temple, while Cambyses paid homage to the Egyptian gods after his conquest of their land. Local rulers were frequently confirmed in their power after conquest by the Persians, remain-

[3] R. G. Kent, *Old Persian* (New Haven, 1950), 131.

ing rulers in their own right side by side with the royal governors or satraps, or sometimes acting as satraps themselves.

The system of satrapies by which the central government controlled the diverse provinces of the empire was considerably advanced over previous organizations. The geographical division of the satrapies and the tax system were continued by the Greeks after Alexander's conquest of the empire. There was also a kind of central secret police, the "Eyes and Ears of the King," whose duty was to keep an eye on the satraps as well as to inform the king of any suspicious signs of rebellion. To assist the royal officers in carrying out their duties, there was created a postal system of rapid couriers, restricted to government use. The fast-riding horsemen were able to cover great distances by an excellent system of roads, the most famous of which was the royal road from Sardis to Susa, and by the posthouses at regular intervals where a messenger could change horses and receive provisions.

The bureaucracy greatly aided the process of fusing Iranians and other peoples in a unified culture. The Achaemenids used the Semitic Aramaic language as an official tongue, and it became the *lingua franca* of the empire. The Indians and other peoples of the East took the Aramaic alphabet and adapted it to their own needs during the Achaemenid period. Everywhere the armies of the great king went, there the Achaemenid bureaucracy was planted with all of the concomitants of administration—military, financial, and judicial —and communication with other provinces was insured by the official language.

One of the less known achievements of Darius is his introduction of coinage on a world scale. Coinage had been in use only a short time before Darius, probably originating in Lydia, but it was the Achaemenid king who revolutionized the economy of his empire by putting it on a money rather than a barter basis. The Elamite clay tablets found at Persepolis by University of Chicago archaeologists give enlightening proof of this revolution during his reign.

It is impossible to discuss the Achaemenid army in any

detail, but the core of the military establishment was the so-called 10,000 "Immortals," who supplied the bodyguard of the king and kept their number always at 10,000. In time of war large contingents from the various provinces gathered, each with their own weapons and manner of fighting. The navy was for the most part managed by the Phoenicians, but as we know was not too successful against the Greeks.

The Achaemenids had a reputation for justice and for imposing severe sentences on evildoers. On one occasion, we are told, a judge who had accepted a bribe was flayed alive and his skin made into a covering for his bench, whereupon his son was appointed in his stead and admonished to guide his actions by the knowledge of where he was sitting.[4] The sons of nobles were taught to shoot with a bow, ride a horse, and to speak the truth. Telling the truth had a prominent place in the ethical code of the ancient Persians.

A discussion of the Achaemenids would be incomplete without mention of the religion of the prophet Zoroaster, for he probably flourished in the eastern part of the Achaemenid empire about the time of Cyrus. As happens with most prophets Zoroaster seems to have had a difficult time at first, when he was ridiculed and cast out of his homeland. Fleeing eastward he found a patron, and this turned his luck; soon his religion was on a firm basis. Scholars have written in great detail about the Zoroastrian religion, discussing questions of the date of the prophet and the nature of his religion, but unfortunately few agree. Although all religious books tend at times to be abstract and difficult to follow, the Bible and even the Quran are models of clarity in comparison with the Avesta. The text has been corrupted in transmission through the centuries, but even the Avestan language itself is quite difficult. Another complicating factor is the syncretic nature of Zoroastrianism, at least after Achaemenid times. The Indo-Aryan pantheon and many ancient practices found their way into the Zoroastrian faith, while the rites and beliefs of the Magi, the priests who were prominent among the Medes, were additional elements in the mixture.

[4] Herodotus V, 25.

The place of Zoroastrianism in the Achaemenid empire is uncertain, but it exerted a strong influence on other religions, including Judaism, Christianity, and Islam. Thus the concept of a dualism of good and evil seems to be a prime feature of Zoroastrianism which influenced other religions. There seems little doubt that Zoroastrianism must be considered one of the world's great religions, imposing in its ethical standards, and a source of ideas for followers of other faiths in later times.

THE CONQUEST OF ALEXANDER THE GREAT

The later Achaemenid kings were not great leaders or organizers as were their predecessors. Under Xerxes, son of Darius, the Greeks demonstrated that the large Achaemenid armies could be defeated by a small well-disciplined force. Inner weaknesses in the large empire appeared when court intrigues had already weakened the central authority. Revolts in the provinces were put down with difficulty by bribery and intrigue or by the use of Greek mercenaries. When the last Darius ascended the throne, there seemed some hope of a revival of central authority throughout the empire, but unfortunately for Iran a young military genius had appeared in Macedonia who was to change the face of the world.

Alexander, it seems, was not only impressed with the military possibilities of conquest but held a belief that the Orient and Occident could be united to form a world state even greater than the Achaemenid empire, with cultural as well as political unity. The spread of Hellenic culture in the wake of Alexander's conquest by the planting of Greek military colonies and cities throughout the Orient must have been a really great undertaking.What can be more fascinating than the story of the Bactrian Greeks, those remnants of Alexander's army who carved out a kingdom for themselves in Central Asia and then moved down to the plains of India, for the first time bringing Greek thought and culture into contact with the civilization of India. It was these Greeks who gave the Buddhists a model for their sculptured Buddha figures, based on statues of Apollo, which eventually spread to China where it was transformed to conform to Far Eastern tastes. One would like to think that the ideas of Plato reached India by this means and influenced Indian philosophers.

The books which have been written about Alexander the Great fill many shelves in a library, and certainly his life story has had an extraordinary attraction for later conquerors —for Caesar and Napoleon to mention only two. In Iran, however, Alexander was and is regarded as an evil magician with two horns who wrought much harm in the land.

After the premature death of Alexander in 323 B.C., his empire fell to pieces, but they were Hellenic pieces. Greek kings continued to rule in Asia and Greek culture developed and spread. Iran too underwent a "Hellenization," though perhaps less than Mesopotamia or Syria. It is difficult to gauge the influence of Hellenism in Iran even from the vantage point of the twentieth century, but it must have been comparable to the influence of the West today. How else would the contact of the Greek genius be with such receptive people as the Persians? We see today the Greek influence in art objects from this period, and even in distant Baluchistan it is reported that a well preserved amphitheater built by Alexander's army exists to this day. But these are only isolated indications of the influence of Greek culture on the population of Iran. Unfortunately our sources for this period of Iran's history are scanty indeed, more so than under the Achaemenids. Archaeology has been of singularly little help; so in respect to our knowledge this can be called the dark period of Iranian history. The curtain does not lift until the establishment of the Sassanian dynasty, but that is over five centuries after the death of Alexander. What happened during this time?

Politically, the Greeks in Iran were partially replaced within a century after Alexander by an Iranian people, the Parthians, who conquered the plateau from their homeland to the north. Culturally the Parthians adopted the Hellenism of their predecessors and at times seemed more royalist than the king in this regard. The movement of the Parthians into Iran coincided with other migrations from Central Asia into what is now Afghanistan and northern India. The Greek kingdoms there too lost their independence. In Iran there was a series of barbarian invasions comparable to those which overthrew the Roman Empire years later. But just as a new civilization rose from the ashes of Rome compounded of Christianity, old Roman traditions, and barbarian practices, so in Iran eventually a new composite of Hellenism, old Iranian culture, and Zoroastrianism developed. Under the later Parthians the Zoroastrian religion was already becoming an organized state religion, later to be perfected by the Sassanians.

The Parthian period of Iran's history is almost a blank, in great measure because of the desire of their successors to eradicate the memory of the Parthians from their subjects. In fact the Sassanians went so far as to falsify history by subtracting some 200 years from the length of rule of the Parthians. In Islamic times this fraud of the Sassanians was revealed, but so much had it penetrated the common people that it entered the Persian epic tradition in the *Shah Name* and elsewhere.

The Parthians established a feudal state which lasted until 226 A.D., and it is probable that many of the features of feudalism and chivalry in Europe—for example, the coat-of-arms—came from the Parthians. The Parthians were the first to administer a crushing defeat to the victorious Roman armies when in 53 B.C. the consul Crassus lost his life to Parthian horsemen with bows. This defeat convinced the Romans that they would have to make use of cavalry, so they instituted in their army heavily mailed horsemen, the *clibanari*. The Parthians remained the unconquerable enemy of the Roman Empire until they were supplanted by an even more formidable empire.

SASSANIAN IRAN

The first ruler of the new dynasty, Ardashir Papakan, had been a feudal lord or vassal of the Parthian king in the province of Fars. About 220 A.D. he revolted, much as Cyrus had risen against Cyaxares over 800 years previously, and after several battles won an undisputed victory. The last Parthian king, Artabanus III, was killed in 226, and a new dynasty held sway.

The Sassanians, so-named like the Achaemenids after an eponymous ancestor, sought to re-establish the empire of pre-Alexandrian days, and to further this, in their official propaganda they did everything possible to discredit their Phil-Hellene predecessors. The new dynasty was to be one hundred per cent Iranian. Its advent marked a new spirit in both internal and foreign affairs. In place of a loose feudal regime the Sassanians created a centralized state and at the same time a strong state church. Furthermore, under the Sassanians society became more fixed in classes or castes. In fact the division of the people into four general classes of priests, warriors, bureaucracy, and common people—both peasants and artisans—parallels the caste system of India, although it seems never to have been so rigid as the castes. The nobles and princes were probably above the four-fold division of people, for they too had various ranks.

The most important innovation of the Sassanians, however, was the state church with a veritable pope at the head, the *mobadan-mobad*, chief of the *mobads* or Magi, the priests. The empire was divided into ecclesiastical districts, and a regular priestly hierarchy existed. That the *mobadan-mobad* had great influence and could wield enormous power is indicated by the rock-carved inscriptions of the religious leader during the reign or Shapur (Sapor), son of Ardashir, and his successors. This man, Kartir by name, was unknown to history before the still incomplete decipherment of his inscriptions, even though he was probably the man most responsible for the creation of a strong state church. In one of his inscriptions, on a stone structure at Naqsh-i-Rustam near Persepolis, after a recital of his deeds which does not stint his self-esteem, he says (in rough translation), "This inscription was written by me for this purpose, that whosoever in the future sees [these] royal records, rescripts, or other inscriptions, he shall know that I am Kartir, who under

Shapur, King of Kings, was called Kartir the *ehrpat,* and under Ohrmizd, King of Kings, and Varahran, King of Kings, was called Kartir, Ahuramazda's *mobad,* and under Varahran, King of Kings, Varahran's son, I was called savior of Varahran's soul and Ahuramazda's *mobad,* and whosoever sees and reads this inscription may he be sincere and true to the gods, to the nobles, and to himself, just as I have been . . ."

One must remember that under the Sassanians the Zoroastrian religion, like later Islam, greatly influenced the daily life of the believer. In ritual this was manifested in the fire cult, which was of such an importance that later writers have designated the Zoroastrians as fire worshippers. It seems that each king, on his inauguration, instituted with great ceremony his regnal fire, which was, so to speak, the symbol of his reign. Then there were lesser fires kept ever burning in temples or special edifices erected for the purpose in towns and villages. Three "great" fires existed, dedicated to the classes of priests, warriors, and farmers respectively, and these three shrines were more venerated than others. Thus there was in effect an important fire ritual in Zoroastrianism, which if not invented by the Sassanians was certainly greatly developed by them.

War with Rome was begun by Ardashir and continued by his son, Shapur, who about 260 A.D. inflicted a great defeat on the Roman army, taking the emperor Valerian captive. This memorable event was recorded on a number of still extant rock reliefs in southern Iran. Large numbers of Roman prisoners were settled by Shapur in Khuzistan, where they built three large dams at Shustar, Dizful, and Karkha as part of an extensive irrigation system. Parts of these dams still exist, and Persians say that if they were rebuilt on the same sites irrigation would again flourish in the province and its neglected agriculture would be restored.

After Shapur the empire declined; the Romans regained lost ground and the priests and nobles asserted themselves against the royal power. It remained for a reformer king, Khusrau (Chosroes) Anushirvan "of immortal soul" (531-

579), to restore kingly prerogatives by a series of reforms. The tax system was renovated and land surveyed and assessed as the prime source of revenue. The army too underwent change, for knighthood was now in flower, as it soon was to become in Europe, and Iranian knights formed the backbone of the army. Frontier garrisons were organized and captives from the hardy peoples of the northern steppes were settled in the border provinces facing the Romans to provide a permanent defense against the enemy.

Wars with the Romans, rather with the Byzantines who had replaced the Romans, continued after Khusrau's death, and as a result both countries suffered grievously from invasions. Under a later king, a namesake of Khusrau, Persian troops conquered Jerusalem, Alexandria in Egypt, and by 619 had reached the Bosphorus across from Constantinople. It seemed as though at last the Achaemenid empire would be restored. But the fortunes of war changed, and the new Byzantine emperor Heraclius invaded Iran and soon reversed the positions. This was in 628, six years after an event in the heart of Arabia which went unnoticed by both Persians and Byzantines, the flight of an Arab from Mecca to the city of Medina. For the days of Sassanian Iran were numbered, while ruler succeeded ruler in rapid succession amidst revolts against the crown and much bloodshed.

The Sassanians are honored today in Iran as the last native dynasty before the Arab invasion which changed the course of history so much. The present dynasty took its name from the Middle Persian language of Sassanian Iran—Pahlevi. Under Reza Shah, when attempts were made to reform the Persian vocabulary, purging it of Arabic words, the Pahlevi language provided many substitutes. Sassanian motifs were frequently copied in art and architecture and the influence of Sassanian Iran is still alive in the Iran of today.

THE ARAB CONQUEST AND ITS AFTERMATH

Iran has suffered numerous invasions from Central Asia throughout her history, but none of the Semitic waves rose over the plateau until the Arabs came in the 7th century of our era. We are not concerned with the reasons for the appearance of Muhammad, whether it was overpopulation, desiccation and famine, or other causes which brought the Arab armies out of the wastes of Arabia, but the religious fervor of the Muslims and the weakness of their opponents led to vast conquests. One may believe that there was a kind of religious bankruptcy of Zoroastrianism in Iran and Christianity in the Semitic world, else the Muslims would not have made the progress they did. In any event the Arabs came not only with a new religion but a new society, a new state, in short a revolutionary force which fed and grew on successes.

The rapidity with which the Arabs conquered Iran after defeating the Sassanian armies in a series of battles—the last important one was at Nihavand in 641—is remarkable, for the imperial armies of both Iran and Byzantium were defeated by smaller numbers of rude tribesmen. Most history books describe the Muslim invasion as a horde of fanatics with Quran in one hand and sword in the other, asking the conquered people to choose. This view is quite false, but one should not swing to the other extreme and conclude that the Muslims were motivated by plunder and political power and had no missionary spirit. We know that there were large areas in Iran with few Muslims in them even 300 years after the conquest. The Zoroastrian church, once it lost official support, fell apart rapidly, but Zoroastrians continued to flourish cut off from each other by groups of newly converted Muslims. Contrary to Islam, Zoroastrianism was not a missionary religion, and the rather exclusive nature of the latter aided conversion to the new more democratic faith.

The Arabs did not replace the governmental organization of the Sassanians, and for several generations after the conquest they continued to employ Pahlevi in the official records and to strike coins with the effigy of the last Sassanian king, Yezdegird III. But just as with the Achaemenids, so the Arab rulers had to adopt a *lingua franca* for the many lands over which they ruled. Arabic was the natural choice, not only because it was the tongue of the conquerors and of their holy book, but a wonderfully flexible instrument which developed considerably after contact with Greek philosophy and Persian ideas. Arabic rivalled and even surpassed Latin in the Middle Ages as the language of science and learning. Persians contributed much to this; for example, the earliest grammarians of Arabic, such as Sibawaih, were Persians, since they had to learn the foreign language and establish its rules of grammar. The roll of Iranians who gained fame by their writings in Arabic is long, including such names as Avicenna, al-Biruni, Rhazes, and al-Ghazzali, who reconciled orthodoxy and mysticism in the Islamic religion.

The 'Umayyad Caliphate was essentially an "Arab empire" with its capital in Damascus and its face towards the Mediterranean Sea. Syria was the homeland of the caliphs and the source of their support, even though the empire continued to expand. Under the 'Umayyads, the armies of Islam reached and crossed the Pyrenees about 718 A.D., while in the east they conquered territory to the steppes of Central Asia and to the Indus River. Although at first the Arab warriors were not supposed to acquire land, it was only natural that they should reap benefits from the conquests, and soon they became a landed aristocracy ruling over large numbers of non-Muslims as well as new converts. The latter—Egyptians, Persians, Syrians, and others who had become Muslims —found that they did not attain the same rank as the Arab Muslim. In fact discrimination by special favors and in taxation by the government caused much dissatisfaction among the non-Arab Muslim converts. When the non-Arab Muslims outnumbered the Arabs, the situation became critical.

There were many reasons for the fall of the 'Umayyad Caliphate besides the discontent of the non-Arab Muslims; the Shiites were enemies of the established regime, while many Arabs resented their own aristocracy. Then there were the inter-tribal feuds among the Arabs themselves, which weakened the authority of the government. Nevertheless, by one means or another the 'Umayyads maintained their power until 750, when the 'Abbasids seized power from the Syrians.

There were many enemies of the 'Umayyads, but they could never unite for common action until an excellent organizer came on the scene, a Persian Muslim called Abu Muslim. As a lieutenant of one 'Abbas, a descendant of an uncle of Muhammad who was anti-'Umayyad, Abu Muslim won over the people of Khurasan to revolt. The Arab tribes which had been settled in Khurasan to keep the peace were fighting each other, so the 'Abbasids had a clear field to rally support to themselves. All who hated the 'Umayyads flocked to serve under the black flags of the 'Abbasids and the leadership of Abu Muslim, and he led them to victory.

Some scholars have explained the 'Abbasid revolt as an uprising of the Persians against the Arabs, and maintain that the new caliphate was Persian rather than Arab. While it is true that the new rulers established their capital in Iraq and were greatly influenced by Sassanian customs in court, the 'Abbasids were Arabs and did not hold power on the basis of the dominance of any race or people. The 'Abbasid revolt was rather a social and economic revolt against the dominant group of landowners who supported the 'Umayyad regime.

The new dynasty was pro-Persian insofar as Sassanian Persian influences were strong; the capital was at Baghdad, in land which had been under Sassanian rule; and unlike the 'Umayyads the 'Abbasids were less concerned with the Mediterranean and more with Iran and Central Asia. The Arab kingdom, ruled by a caliph who acted much as a tribal chieftain, gave way to a despotic empire with a caliph almost divine, isolated from his subjects and passing on the office to his son. Pre-Islamic Persian forms of court etiquette and features of the old Sassanian bureaucracy increased in importance under the 'Abbasids. It is apparent that in spite of the leveling process of a democratic religion such as Islam, the Persians maintained much of their stratified social system, a survival from Sassanian times. The Persian nobility maintained their privileges, making their peace with the Arabs, and even at times obtaining the support of the Arabs in keeping the lower classes in line. For example, in the

History of Bukhara by Narshakhi, it is related that the ruler of Bukhara, who was not a Muslim, complained to the Muslim governor that some of his subjects had accepted Islam in order to avoid paying the poll tax levied on non-Muslims, and that they were causing disorder in the province because of this. As a result, the new converts were arrested by Arab troops and turned over to the ruler of Bukhara for execution.[5]

As a result of the growth of Persian influence under the 'Abbasids, it was only natural that uprisings against Arab or Muslim authority should occur in Iran. The end of the 8th century is filled with such revolts, most of them religious as well as political, but none of them successful. Among the leaders were such interesting religious figures as Sinbad the Magian, who sought to revive a new Zoroastrianism but was killed in 756, and Muqanna the veiled prophet of Khurasan, hero of Moore's *Lalla Rookh,* who proclaimed himself the messiah of the Persian people. His rebellion was put down with difficulty in 780.

Islam soon became the dominant religion in Iran and subsequent revolts lost their religious character and became political. The first of the "Persian kingdoms" to be established under the 'Abbasid Caliphate was that of the governors of Khurasan, the Tahirid family. Although they paid allegiance to the caliphs, the caliphs in their turn, after 822, appointed only members of the family as governors, giving the dynasty a hereditary character. Although we know little about the court of the Tahirids at Nishapur, it is probable that they patronized Persian poets and artists much as later dynasties did, even though nothing has survived from Tahirid times. In effect the power of the caliphs had ended forever in Iran; hereafter only lip service was paid to the head of the Islamic world; and this primarily because of the regard for the caliph as a religious rather than a political figure. In the West—Spain, North Africa, and Egypt—even the caliph's religious supremacy was not recognized. The first indications of the separation of religious and political functions in the Islamic world had appeared and this was to start lengthy

[5] Ed. Charles Schefer (Paris, 1892), 58.

and learned discussions among the Muslim savants on the nature of the Islamic state, which ended under the Seljuqs (Seljuks) in the political theory of the sultan in charge of temporal affairs, while the caliph concerned himself with religious and legal affairs. Naturally the relations of caliph with sultan were at times awkward and even conflicting, and only with the end of the caliphate itself was the problem of dual authority resolved.

The last Tahirid, Muhammad ibn Tahir, was defeated in battle by an army of rebels from the province of Seistan led by a coppersmith called Yaqub ibn Laith. This revolt was in no sense a Persian popular revolt against the caliphate but simply a movement against the authority of the Tahirids, and it was entirely successful. Yaqub extended his sway over much of Iran and part of Afghanistan after his defeat of the last Tahirid in 872. But the Saffarids in turn gave way to a more important dynasty, the Samanids, who from their capital at Bukhara in Central Asia soon conquered most of the Saffarid domain. The founder of Samanid power was one Ismail who died in 907.

Under the Samanids Persian literature was revived for the first time since the Sassanians. The Samanid rulers were conscious of their heritage as a noble Iranian family, and they sought to link their lineage with the Sassanian ruling house in order to appear as successors of the pre-Islamic dynasty. Some of the Persian nobility had undoubtedly migrated from Fars and western Iran to Central Asia rather than come to terms with the Arabs. They provided the impetus for the cultural flowering of Bukhara and Samarqand under the Samanids, for the local population spoke Sogdian, an Iranian language to be sure, but not Persian. The influence of the refugees must have been very strong, for Persian displaced Sogdian as the language of Bukhara and Samarqand.

The Samanids were great patrons not only of poets but also of scientists, theologians (since the Samanids were strict Sunnite Muslims), and artists. Avicenna and Rhazes were encouraged and honored by Samanid rulers, and the earliest great Persian poets, the lyricist Rudagi and Daqiqi, who began the great Persian epic the *Shah Name,* both lived in Bukhara. One of the first prose works in Persian, a translation of the history of Tabari from Arabic, was written at the Samanid court. Here the transition from a Zoroastrian to an Islamic Persian culture was complete; models were set in literary forms and adhered to strictly throughout the centuries to the present day. Although it was a national Persian revival in Samanid domains, Islam was everywhere dominant.

At the same time that the Sunnite Samanids were fostering Persian culture in eastern Iran, a dynasty of Shiite rulers had enlarged their boundaries from Mazanderan on the Caspian Sea coast to include most of western Iran and finally Baghdad itself. This was the dynasty of the Buwayhids, so-named after the founder's family, which lasted until the Seljuq Turks took Baghdad in 1055. The Buwayhids were the first important dynasty in Iran which was Shiite, a religion which was later to become the national religion of the country. They also adopted the pre-Islamic Iranian title of Shahinshah, "king of kings," and sought to attach their genealogy to the Sassanian royal house. Although the 'Abbasid caliphs were Sunnites, the Buwayhid rulers who usurped the caliph's temporal powers thought it politically wise not to replace the caliph with a Shiite candidate but to leave him in office. Nonetheless the caliphs had little to say and were made and deposed at Buwayhid orders. The prestige of the caliphal office, however, kept it alive, for an attempt to abolish the office would have created an uproar all over the Islamic world.

THE TURKISH INVASIONS

The Iranian kingdoms were destined to fall to Turkish tribes from Central Asia. The Turkish invasions of Iran may be compared with the Germanic invasions of the Roman Empire in the fourth and fifth centuries A.D. For several centuries before 1000, Turkish mercenaries had served as auxiliaries in the caliph's guard. They also had enlisted in the armies of the Samanids, while pagan Turks were sold in the slave markets of Baghdad. So Turks were no strangers in this part of the world. Like the German mercenaries in the Roman Empire, the Turks began to play the role of a privileged guard. Already in the ninth century the Turkish guard of the caliph nominated and deposed their masters; in fact the excesses of the Turkish guards prompted a number of the caliphs to maintain their courts at the newly built city of Samarra to the north of Baghdad. The military prowess of the Turks became well known, and it was not long before their numbers increased in the military forces everywhere in the Near East. The final stage was the creation of Turkish states on the heels of invasion, much as the Germanic states were erected on the ruins of the Roman Empire.

The first of these states was created at the expense of the Samanids. Alptegin, a Turkish slave of the Samanid rulers, had risen to high office and was appointed governor of Khurasan in 961. He soon decided to act on his own and abandoned the Samanids to conquer for himself a small kingdom in Afghanistan, with his capital at Ghazna. He was succeeded by his son-in-law Subuktegin, but the most famous ruler of this dynasty was the latter's son, known in history as Mahmud of Ghazna. Mahmud defeated the last of the Samanids in 999 and took over most of their domains in eastern Iran. A strict and even fanatic Sunnite Muslim, he is credited with spreading Islam by the sword in India in the wake of his extensive raids into the sub-continent, where he collected enormous booty. Mahmud felt himself the successor of the Samanids in every way, for he invited scholars and poets to his court at Ghazna, which outshone Bukhara in its assembly of learned men. It was here that Firdausi completed the *Shah Name* begun by Daqiqi and al-Biruni passed considerable time.

Afterwards, not only in Iran but elsewhere in the Near East, Turks established kingdoms to the extent that from this time the business of ruling became a prerogative of this hardy and warlike people. It became a commonplace among the peoples of the Near East that the Turks excelled in governing as the Arabs in religion and the Persians in the arts. This has been compared to the relative positions of the Germans, French, and Italians in Medieval Europe by some scholars who say that the first were concerned with the *imperium*, the second with the *magisterium*, and the last with the *sacerdotium*. Of course the Turks borrowed much from Iran; the language at court was Persian rather than Turkish, and the Persian bureaucracy was adopted by the Turkish rulers. Turkish sultans for centuries continued to use Persian as the language of state even in non-Iranian lands. Still the Turks did make an impression on Iran, much of which is difficult to measure, yet which persists to the present.

The Seljuq Turks were the successors of the rulers of Ghazna, but they soon established a much greater empire, extending from Central Asia to the Mediterranean. The names of the sons of Seljuq, chief of the Turkish tribe in Central Asia before it moved into Iran, usually given as Israil, Mikhail, Yunus (Jonah), and Musa, suggest that the Turks had been in contact with Nestorian Christians or followers of Judaism in the south Russian kingdom of the Khazars. In any case, when the Seljuqs moved south they were converted to Islam and, like most new converts, were stronger in their faith than the settled people over whose lands they moved. With a strict and efficient military organization characteristic of the tribes of the Central Asian steppes, the Seljuqs carved an empire for themselves at the expense of the Ghazanvid rulers and the Buwayhids.

Under the Seljuqs the functions of the heads of state and church were separated, for the Seljuq leader Tughril in 1057 received a document from the caliph granting him secular rule over all of the lands which had been granted to the caliph by God. The Seljuqs were worthy heirs of the caliph's temporal power, for "they put a new life into the expiring zeal of the Muslims, drove back the re-encroaching Byzantines, and bred up a generation of fanatical Mohammadan warriors to whom more than to anything else, the Crusaders owed their repeated failure."[6] The battle of Manzikert in 1071 marks an important date in world history, for after the defeat of the Byzantine army by the Seljuq Sultan Alp Arslan, Anatolia was opened to Turkish conquest.

What happened to Iran under the Seljuqs, and why did Iran maintain its identity while Anatolia became Turkish? One must go back in history, for it is important to remember that Iranian society remained much the same under Islam as before. It is true that Islam at first appealed to the lower classes, as our sources, especially the chronicles of Persian cities, tell us; but the nobles—the great landlords or *dihqans*, as they were called—maintained their position and became Muslims only if it was to their advantage. In many cases they continued to exercise authority though remaining Zoroastrians, as we know from several city chronicles. Changes in rulers usually meant only a change in the recipient of taxes, and the bureaucracy was content to continue working for new masters. The Seljuqs maintained this pattern and left affairs in Persian hands. The *vezir* or prime minister of Sultan Alp Arslan (1063-1072) and his son Malikshah (1072-1091) was the famous Nizam al-Mulk, the author of a book on government which was highly regarded by his contemporaries. He was a Persian, a patron of the arts and an excellent administrator. The story of his boyhood friendship with Omar Khayyam and with the founder of the sect of Assassins, Hasan-i-Sabbah, is more legend than fact, but under him all kinds of scholars flourished and wrote. Iran then conquered the Seljuqs culturally. In Anatolia, on the other hand, the population was Christian and hostile to Islam; and it was a Seljuq policy to send unruly Turkish nomads against the Byzantines or the Christian kingdoms of Georgia and Armenia to turn then away from Islamic lands. By this means Iran was spared the inundation which Anatolia suffered. It is also significant to remember that in effect Anatolia was not only Turkicized but Islamized and also Iranized.

[6] S. Lane-Poole, *The Mohammadan Dynasties* (London, 1894), 150.

It was Nizam al-Mulk who advocated and realized a feudal system of land grants to military officers, thus integrating the Turkish chieftains into the Persian landed aristocracy. One historian of this period says, "It had been the custom to collect money from the country and pay it to the troops, and no one had previously had a fief. Nizam al-Mulk saw that the money was not coming in from the country on account of its disturbed state and that the yield was uncertain because of its disorder. Therefore he divided it among the troops in fiefs, assigning to them both the yield and the revenue. Then interest in its development increased greatly, and it returned rapidly to a flourishing state."[7]

A word is necessary about the Ismailis in Iran, the followers of Hasan-i-Sabbah, who flourished during the Seljuq period. The Ismailis, a Shiite sect also known as the "Seveners," were followers of Ismail, one of the two sons of the sixth Imam Ja'far. They refused to recognize the other son and his descendants to the twelfth imam as did the great majority of Shiites. Their leader, the "Old Man of the Mountains," established his sect of fanatics in strong mountain fortresses throughout Iran and used assassination as a means to political power and influence. He instituted a reign of terror by sending his followers, hashish addicts—whence their name "assassins"—to murder prominent political leaders who opposed the Ismailis. Nizam al-Mulk supported the orthodox Sunnite forces against this Shiite sect, and as a result was murdered by one of the assassins. Sunnite Islam, however, was upheld in the Seljuq domains. The assassins were not extirpated until the Mongols captured their chief stronghold and killed their grand master. The Aga Khan is the chief of the Ismaili sect today, small in numbers and peacefully inclined.

THE MONGOL CATACLYSM

The Turks became part of the now well-established Islamic civilization and contributed to it, but their suc-

[7] Quoted by B. Lewis, *The Arabs in History* (London, 1950), 148.

cessors, the Mongols, coming from the Far East, were alien to the culture of the Near East. In a sense they were the climax of centuries of invasion into Iran from the Central Asian steppes—the last great wave of Aryans, Scythians, Huns, and Turks. And like their predecessors, the Mongols relied for their military success primarily on iron discipline and swift-moving mounted archers. They were experts in the use of terror and fifth column tactics as a deliberate military policy; indeed many of their battles were won before they were fought because the enemy had been demoralized by frightening tales brought by refugees from the Mongol hordes.

Chinghis (Jenghiz) Khan and his successors created the largest land empire the world has ever known, extending from the China Sea to the plains of Hungary. In 1221 the Mongols invaded Iran, leaving death and destruction in the wake of their armies. But Chinghis Khan did not establish Mongol rule in Persia; this was left to his grandson Hulagu a quarter of a century later. Hulagu conquered Iran and captured Baghdad in 1258, killing the last 'Abbasid Caliph. Iran became the center of a new Mongol dynasty called the Il-Khans by historians. Again—and for the first time since pre-Islamic times—Persia was cut off from the rest of the Near East and her political and cultural ties linked with Central Asia rather than the Mediterranean.

The Il-Khans of Persia were Buddhists or Christians until the reign of Ghazan (1295-1304), who became a Muslim. Although the Mongols destroyed many towns and put to death many Muslims, it was not out of any hatred for Islam but rather as a military policy. After the creation of a Mongol state in Iran they in fact showed themselves quite tolerant of all religions. Nor were the Mongol rulers remiss in encouraging historians and other men of science and letters. We have a considerable number of histories of the Mongols in Persian, including the excellent world history of Rashid al-Din, prime minister of Ghazan, so we are well informed about Mongol rule in Iran. Furthermore we have preserved in the Vatican the letters in Mongolian sent to the pope and the king of France by the Il-Khans, who sought an alliance with European Christians against their common enemy, the Mamelukes of Egypt, who had expelled the last Crusaders from the Holy Land. Nothing came of the attempt to join forces, for the appeal of the Crusades in Europe was already gone and the Mongols had not behaved as possible allies when they invaded Poland and Hungary. The *Pax Mongolica* extending over Asia and Eastern Europe opened the Far East to European travellers such as William of Rubruck and Marco Polo, but the vast empire soon broke into mutually hostile segments, of which Persia was one.

It is difficult to estimate the permanent damage done to Iran—to her cities, irrigation system, and economic life— by the Mongols. However, though the Mongols killed many people and destroyed much property, it would be wrong to ascribe the subsequent decline of Iran solely to the Mongols.

One result of Mongol rule in Iran was the introduction of Far Eastern motifs in art. Both ceramics and miniature painting were greatly influenced by the craftsmanship of Chinese artisans. Typically Chinese landscapes appear in the miniatures, giving a new life to Persian painting. Other Far Eastern inventions appeared in Iran; one was ill-fated, the introduction of paper money in 1294, which had been successful in China but caused a financial crisis in Iran. During Il-Khan rule in Persia the great poet Sa'di lived and wrote in Shiraz, soon followed by Hafiz. Hence Mongol rule was not wholly negative, at least in the cultural sphere.

After the death of the Il-Khan Abu Said in 1335, the Mongol state in Iran fell apart and various princes and chieftains fought among themselves for the pieces. The Mongol armies had long since become more Turkish than Mongol, so when Timur, or Tamerlane as he is sometimes known in the West, appeared on the scene, it was as a leader of primarily Turkish forces. Still, he began his career in the Mongol political tradition with the dream of restoring the great Mongol empire of Chinghis Khan. However, Timur came as a Muslim conqueror into Iran fighting against Muslim princes. In the north he sacked and plundered

Moscow in 1382, but at the same time dealt a death blow to the Mongol state of the "Golden Horde," which opened the way for Russian expansion. In 1398 he invaded India, advancing as far as Delhi, which he captured and plundered. In 1402 he defeated and captured the Ottoman Sultan Bayezit—fresh from his victory over the European Crusaders at Nicopolis—in a battle near the present city of Ankara. This set back the Ottoman timetable of capturing Constantinople. It was on an expedition to conquer China that Timur died in 1405, after having restored much of the original Mongol empire of Chinghis Khan.

Timur, however, was an adventurer who, if anything, exceeded his predecessors in a policy of terror. He is known for the pyramids of heads which he erected, and for various atrocities such as burying alive entire garrisons which had resisted him. At the same time he was a great builder and made a show place of his capital at Samarqand in Central Asia, to which he brought captive artisans and builders. Timur spoke Persian as well as Turkish and as usual played the patron of the arts, favoring the historians who recounted his exploits in ornate Persian prose or verse. In world history Timur's fame cannot rank high since his record of wanton destruction outweighs his constructive achievements.

His son and grandson ruled a much reduced empire including eastern Iran and Turkistan. Shah Rukh with his court at Herat and Ulugh Beg at Samarqand gave a reputation of science and learning to the Timurid family; the latter was a famous astronomer as well as ruler, and his book on astronomy enjoyed great popularity during the following two or three centuries not only in the Orient but also in the Occident. Other Timurid princes were artists or writers to such an extent that the fifteenth century in Iran, just as in contemporary Italy, was a century of cultural flowering, and it has been called the Timurid period of Iran's history. The prevailing style of art and literature was highly ornate— both prose and poetry were florid and somewhat artificial— but some of the masterpieces of Persian painting and poetry were produced at this time. Behzad the painter (ca. 1450-

1536) gave Persian book miniatures their classical expression, and the poet Jami (1414-1492), who lived in Herat, exemplified the current trend towards mysticism in his poems. With political disorders on every side, the Persians turned more to religion, to dervish orders and various sects as a refuge from the ills of the world. But this was to have a political result.

THE GOLDEN AGE OF THE SAFAVIDS

The breakup of Timurid power was followed by the rise of two powers, the Uzbeks (Uzbegs) in Turkistan and the Safavids in Iran. The former were a Turkish tribe who seem to have taken their name from a Khan of the Golden Horde in South Russia, and who moved south to inherit the Timurid legacy. Their first ruler in history was Shaibani Khan, the opponent of Babur who, after his defeat at the hands of the Uzbeks, turned to India, where he created an empire; his eminent successors were known as the Moghul dynasty, which lasted until the English deposed the last Moghul in 1857. The Uzbeks met their match in the Safavid Shah Ismail, though they were not crushed, but remained in the land today known as the Uzbek SSR.

The Safavids began as leaders of a Shiite dervish order in Ardebil, Azerbaijan, but their aspirations turned to politics when the Timurid collapse opened the way for ambitious local princelings. In 1499 their leader Ismail proclaimed himself the leader of all Shiites, and three years later he took the title of Shah. The existence of Iran as a national state may be said to date from this time, but the strength of the state was religion. Ismail would have been just another local ruler of the 16th century in Iran if he had not actively worked for the success of Shiite Islam. One may compare the rise of the Safavids with the Reformation in Europe, for the two movements were similar in many respects. Ismail believed in the necessity of holding political power in order to establish the true faith—that of the twelve imams. The movement was not of Iranian "nationalism," for

Ismail spoke Turkish and he appealed to the Turks of Anatolia as well as to Persians, but the rise of the Ottoman Empire in Anatolia and in the Arab world made the Ottoman Sultans the champions of Sunnite Islam while the Safavids and the Persians became identified with Shiism. In a sense there developed a Shiite "nationalism," but in any case the *basis* for a national state was laid unwittingly by Ismail and crystallized by the course of history which divided the Near East between the Ottomans and the Safavids. Nationalism in the Western sense, of course, did not enter Iran until the end of the 19th or the beginning of the 20th century.

It was inevitable that the two great powers would clash, and in 1514 Sultan Selim defeated Shah Ismail, with the Ottoman artillery playing the major role in the victory. Ismail, however, maintained his state and indeed established the social and political framework upon which the present-day Iranian state rests.

Ismail died in 1524, only 37 years old, and was followed by his mediocre son Tahmasp, who ruled for 52 years. Under his grandson, Shah 'Abbas (1587-1629), the Safavid state reached its apogee and became a truly Persian rather than a Turkish state. For Ismail had been a priest-king relying for his support on his religious followers, primarily Turks, who were called *Qizilbash*, "red heads" after their headgear. Ismail had created a state church, much as the Sassanians had done with Zoroastrianism in pre-Islamic times. By the time of Shah 'Abbas, Shiite Islam had become identified with Iran, and the *Qizilbash* had renounced all ties with the Sunnite Ottoman Turks and had become Persians. Likewise the feudal character of rule so characteristic of the time of the Seljuq Turks and the Mongols had given way to a strong central power based on religion, with almost a divine right of kings. The entire development of Safavid rule resembles the transition from the Parthian to the Sassanian empire over a millennium before.

Shah 'Abbas the Great had to fight many battles in Iran to consolidate his rule, but once he had unified his land he turned against the Uzbeks to the northeast, who had been raiding in Khurasan. He was completely successful and then turned west against his arch-foes, the Ottomans, from whom he captured Baghdad in 1624. The frontiers of Iran were secured, so Shah 'Abbas could devote himself to the encouragement of trade and the pursuit of the arts.

Throughout Iran, even in the heart of the desert, are remains of countless caravansarais, and if one asks who built them, the answer will invariably be Shah 'Abbas. Many of the bazaars in Iranian cities, especially in Isfahan, owe their organization to Shah 'Abbas, who was very energetic in the furthering of trade and commerce. Perhaps his most impressive monument is the city of Isfahan itself. He established his capital in Isfahan and in 1598 started building the structures which today delight the eye and have brought forth the remark among Persians, "half the world is Isfahan." In the center of the city he made an open area almost 1,500 feet long, where polo was played or races held. The king watched from a large pavilion, the entrance to his gardens, called Ali Kapu, the "Sublime Porte." Across the square was the small, exquisite mosque of Shaikh Lutfullah, father-in-law of Shah 'Abbas. Covered with even more beautiful tile work than the much larger mosque of the Shah nearby, the smaller mosque is the masterpiece of Safavid architecture. Isfahan gloried in other Safavid buildings, as well as parks, gardens, and bridges, all of which charmed the European envoys, who came to the court of the "Great Sophy." Accounts have been left by the Frenchman Tavernier, the English Sherley brothers, Thomas Herbert, and many others. Anthony Sherley says of Isfahan, "Shortly after this (new year's day, 1590) the Shah began to embellish this city, which was destined to become the most beautiful in all Persia. . . . It was not, however, until March, 1598, that 'Abbas declared Ispahan officially the new capital."[8]

Under the Safavids Europe rediscovered Iran, for, while

[8] E. D. Ross, ed. *Sir Anthony Sherley and his Persian Adventure* (London, 1933), 17.

it was true that Venetian and Genoese merchants had maintained trade relations with the country in Mongol and Timurid times, only in Safavid times did ambassadors arrive at the court in Isfahan. The reign of Shah 'Abbas coincided with that of Elizabeth in England, Akbar in India, and the rise of Muscovy to the north. The European powers were seeking aid from the Persians against their common enemy the Ottoman Turks, and in this they were not disappointed. Thus Iran, in a way, played a part in the defense of Europe against the Turks.

NADIR SHAH AND HIS SUCCESSORS

As is so frequently the case with great rulers, Shah 'Abbas was followed by a series of weak and ineffective Shahs. Nevertheless the kingdom was able to continue on its own energy with the bureaucracy and with the loyalty to the Safavid dynasty which 'Abbas had created. But inevitably one of the revolts against the Shah succeeded, and in 1722 Isfahan, the capital, was captured by an Afghan army led by a chieftain who had proclaimed his independence from the Safavids. The capture of Isfahan roused the Safavid followers and especially a Turkish officer who rallied forces to drive out the Afghans. This he did and in 1736 had himself crowned Shah in place of the Safavid prince. Nadir Shah was not only a Turk of the Afshar tribe but a Sunnite. His attempts to re-establish the Sunnite rites in Iran failed, for the Shiite faith had become too deeply imbedded in the people to uproot. Nadir Shah was not content to restore the Safavid boundaries; he looked for new fields to conquer. In 1739 he invaded India and took tremendous booty from the Moghul at Delhi, including the famous Koh-i-Noor diamond and the famous peacock throne encrusted with jewels. His armies were next turned against Bukhara and Samarqand, which he conquered, and then in the Caucasus area he made gains against the Georgians and encroaching Russians.

Nadir Shah required great sums of money for his conquests and as his power grew he became more suspicious of those around him. He caused the crown prince to be blinded because of suspected intrigue. His tyranny increased so that in 1747 at last a group of his officers murdered him in his tent. So ended Iran's last great conqueror, a man who had grown almost insane with power and suspicion, but who at least had cleared Iran of her enemies even though she was left in a weakened condition.

Like a last flowering of the culture of the Safavid period, the rule of Karim Khan Zend in Shiraz brought an end to an epoch. Under the Qajars the European powers were to interfere in the internal affairs of Iran and change the pattern of her history. Karim Khan ruled Iran, except for the province of Khurasan, from 1750 to 1779. His capital was at Shiraz, and what Shah 'Abbas was to Isfahan, Karim Khan was to Shiraz. He erected buildings in Shiraz, and won the hearts of the inhabitants of that city so that his memory is revered there even today. Unfortunately his kingdom scarcely survived his death.

The Qajars were a Turkish tribe whose leaders gained power first in northern Iran and then over the entire country. The first ruler of the new dynasty was a eunuch, Aga Muhammad, a classical example of a bloodthirsty tyrant. Luckily his tyranny was cut short by his murder, and he was succeeded by a weak nephew, Fath 'Ali Shah, who ruled from 1797 to 1834. It was under his rule that Russia first intervened effectively in Persian affairs and set the stage for the recent history of Iran.

3

The West and Oil

MODERN history begins in Iran, as elsewhere in the Near East, with the Napoleonic invasion of Egypt in 1798. This event not only caused England and Russia, two enemies of the emperor-to-be, to counter French influence in the Orient, but it also opened the Near East to an influx of Western ideas and culture. It was comparable to the ancient Greek impact on the Orient following the death of Alexander the Great, .with a parallel emphasis on rationalism and humanism. With the impact of the West, the traditional patterns of life and thought established by Islam were challenged by a secularism and an unbounded faith in the progress of man and science. It seemed, and still seems, to many Persians that the Europeans were arrogant in asserting that the human mind had no bounds and that human reason was a source of truth rather than merely an instrument to prove to doubters the eternal truths of Allah. The conflict of rationalism with authoritarian prophecy is still potent among the intelligentsia in Iran today. But it all started in the 19th century with the invasion by the West, and Russia was first on the scene.

It was the Napoleonic threat to India which aroused British interest in Persia, but the Russians had been dreaming of an outlet to the southern seas since the time of Peter the Great. Peter's army had conquered Baku in 1723, and Russian forces had even landed on the southern shore of the Caspian, but under the great Tsar's successors the Russians withdrew north of the Caucasus. The Russians resumed their advance under Tsar Paul, who was offered the crown of Georgia in 1800 by the dying last ruler of that small state, which he naturally accepted. He created a military force to enforce his authority in Georgia and soon came into conflict with Iran. The new Transcaucasian army of Russia first moved against Erivan, but the Persians at first succeeded in throwing back the invaders.

The diplomatic tangle of the Napoleonic period brought Iran for the first time into the European system of alliances, and the British were the first to conclude a treaty with Fath 'Ali Shah. Sir John Malcolm, on behalf of the East India Company, negotiated a commercial agreement which also promised aid against the French if they should ever reach Iran. The British, however, did nothing to implement the treaty or even show an interest in it, for the Persians were more afraid of the Russians than of the French, while Britain was hoping to enlist Russian aid against Napoleon. So the British treaty went into abeyance. The French took advantage of this and in 1807 signed a treaty of alliance with Iran, following which a military mission was sent to the new Qajar capital at Tehran. But the rapprochement between Napoleon and Tsar Alexander I at Tilsit gave the British another chance, and this time they remained in Iran. The British missions to Iran were composed of some remarkable men, and the result was a series of books which roused the attention of the English-speaking world to Iran and established British interest in the country. James Morier's classic, *Hajji Baba of Ispahan,* was one of the products of these early diplomatic missions.

The Russians shortly replaced the French as the main threat to India and, in a series of minor campaigns in Transcaucasia, defeated the Persian army. The treaty of Gulistan was signed in 1813, giving Russia most of Transcaucasia and exclusive right to maintain a navy on the Caspian Sea. Peace was maintained until 1825 when Russian forces occupied a district in Transcaucasia which had not been assigned to either party in the treaty of Gulistan. War broke out, and after initial Persian successes the Russians carried everything before them, capturing Tabriz in 1827. The Persian forces had fought well, but poor leadership, lack of adequate supplies, and a corrupt government made further resistance hopeless. The following year the treaty of Turkomanchai was signed, which fixed the present boundary between Iran and Russia, required an indemnity from the loser, and imposed the capitulations, which were extra-territorial privileges given Russian subjects in Iran, including freeing them from any Persian legal jurisdiction in case of dispute. In fact it gave the Russian consuls sole responsibility for their subjects in a foreign land. In addition, Russia obtained various trade and commercial privileges.

The treaty of Turkomanchai, according to many Persians, brought a new era in Iran's history; it meant the loss of her independence and made her a pawn in the Anglo-Russian political game. Other European powers were quick to follow the Russians in obtaining capitulatory privileges, and it seemed as though the Persian government had lost all authority in its own house.

The rest of the nineteenth century is the story of the Russian advance in Central Asia and the British counter moves in Afghanistan and Iran. At the Persian court British and Russian diplomats vied with one another to win the confidence of the ruler, which was made easy by the avarice of Fath 'Ali Shah. At his death in 1834 the pro-Russian Muhammad Shah ascended the throne. His reign was spent in vain attempts to take Herat from the Afghans, which brought Iran the strong opposition of the British in India. In 1856, during the reign of Nasr al-Din Shah (1848-1896), however, the Persian army captured Herat, whereupon Britain declared war on Iran and landed troops in the south. After brief fighting, peace was made and Iran evacuated Herat and renounced all claims to Afghanistan.

The Russian advance in Central Asia, held up for a short time by the Crimean War, continued until the oasis of Merv was conquered in 1884 and the present boundary between Iran and Russian Central Asia reached. This advance alarmed the British, and on several occasions war between the great powers seemed imminent, but the boundaries were finally stabilized, though both powers maintained positions of undisguised hostility.

In Iran the despotic court continued to rule as before, with little attention to the new ideas of liberalism abroad and even at home which had been brought back by Persians who had travelled or lived in Europe. The year 1850 saw the execution of a religious heretic called the *Bab,* or "the Gate," at Tabriz. This was the origin of a religious movement which came to be known as Bahaism, named after Baha Allah, a successor of the Bab, and which still has adherents in America and Europe. The followers of the Bab were persecuted in Iran and there were a number of Babi revolts which were cruelly suppressed. Nonetheless the Babis and later Bahais continued to proselytize, for Westernization was beginning to have an influence on educated Persians, who began to question the authority of Shiite Islam and who turned to syncretistic faiths such as Bahaism or to the secularism of the Occident.

The first economic inroad by foreigners was made by Baron Julius de Reuter, a naturalized British subject who in 1872 secured a huge monopoly concession to build railroads, exploit mines, and establish a bank in Iran. Nasr al-Din Shah, however, cancelled the concession after his first trip to Europe the following year, since the Russians opposed the project. Nonetheless, the way for future economic concessions had been prepared, and in 1889 the same Reuter secured a plum in the concession to establish the Imperial Bank of Persia with the right to issue bank notes. In turn the Russians were given the right to open a bank and build a railroad; the latter was finally built during World War I, linking Tabriz with the Russian Transcaucasian system. A tobacco monopoly given to a British firm was rescinded owing to the opposition of the Persian people, who were aroused at the granting of monopoly exploitation to foreigners just to enrich the Shah and pay for his trips to Europe. The Shah spent large sums on his travels and raised money by selling his country's rights to the highest bidder. He wrote an account of his travels which enjoyed considerable popularity among literate Persians. Of the international exhibition of arts and industries held in Paris in 1878, the Shah remarked that to describe all of its wonders he would have to write a book the size of the *Shah Name*.[1] The foreign expeditions of their ruler, however, only brought more bills to the Persian people.

The assassination of the Shah in 1896 revealed a strong opposition to the autocratic rule of the "shadow of God upon earth." It was alleged that the assassin was a partisan of the famous Near Eastern reformer, Jamal al-Din Afghani, who was seeking to modernize and liberalize Islam and bring an end to traditional tyrannies. The discontent of the educated led to the disturbances of 1905 and finally the constitution, a memorable event in Persian history.

THE CONSTITUTIONAL CRISIS

The victory of Japan over Russia made a great impression on the peoples of the Orient. That, as well as the Russian revolution of 1905, exerted an influence on the Persians as well as on the Young Turks, who revolted against their despotic sultan. The autocratic Shah was an anomaly in the twentieth century, even in Iran, and the constitutional crisis surprised but few people. Muzaffar al-Din was just as addicted to foreign travel as his father, but he needed more money and was not loath to increase his debts with the Russians, who gladly advanced the weak ruler funds in return for tariff concessions and other advantages in Iran. The treasury was empty, but the Shah needed money.

Popular discontent was focused on the prime minister and his associates rather than on the person of the Shah, so the first riots and disturbances had for their aim the dismissal of the hated courtiers. To give force to their demands, merchants, religious leaders, students, and others held a sit-down strike in the British Legation compound in Tehran. This strike, an old Persian custom called *bast,* was quite effective, for not only did the Shah dismiss the prime minister, but the strikers obtained a constitution and parliament which they had added to their demands. The first

[1] *A Second Tour in Europe* (London, 1879), 165.

Majlis or National Assembly was convened in October, 1906, and the constitution was signed by the Shah two months later, just before he died.

The new ruler, reactionary Muhammad 'Ali Shah, was determined to suppress the constitution, but he had an aroused populace on his hands. His first attempt to make a *coup d'état* in December 1907 failed, but he was resolved to try again, since the Russians were strongly behind him. The British, on the contrary, had supported the Constitutionalists although they did not favor revolution or removal of the ruler.

In 1907, however, the political situation in Iran was changed by what the Persians regard as the infamous Anglo-Russian convention to divide their country. The text of the agreement reads much like the Anglo-Russian treaty of 1942, when the armies of both powers were occupying Iran. In both, the two powers several times emphasize that the independence and integrity of Iran would be strictly observed. By the agreement of 1907 two zones of influence were created—Russian and British—with a neutral band between them. One country was not to engage in economic or political activities in the zone of the other. The Russians got the lion's share, including all of north and central Persia to Isfahan and Yezd, while the British were content with southeastern Iran, including Kirman and Bandar 'Abbas. The new oil field was in the neutral zone. The defeat of Russia at the hands of Japan and the growing strength of Germany were the main factors bringing the two rivals together. The agreement concerned Afghanistan and Tibet as well as Iran and was one of the pacts which the European powers were forming in choosing sides as the prelude to 1914.

The Persians, of course, were not consulted about the Anglo-Russian accord, and consequently Britain gained a bad reputation which was not improved after World War I or indeed in recent times. The political situation inside the country became worse rather than better, for the Shah felt that now he could act with the tacit if not overt support of the Russians.

The main military force in Iran at this time was the

Cossack brigade, trained and officered by Russians. In June, 1908, the Shah ordered the brigade to disperse the Majlis and its partisans, which task was carried out. Martial law was proclaimed and several of the Shah's most violent opponents were strangled. Tehran was in the Shah's power, but as a result the people of Tabriz revolted and drove the Shah's partisans from the city. The Shah's forces laid siege to Tabriz, but the siege ended in the spring of the following year when Russian troops entered the city to protect foreigners there.

Meanwhile supporters of the constitution assembled in various parts of the country to march on Tehran to restore the constitution and reconstitute the Majlis. In July 1909 the Bakhtiyari tribesmen captured Tehran and deposed the Shah, who had taken refuge in the Russian embassy.

This was not the end of the story, for Muhammad 'Ali in 1911 tried to regain his throne with Russian support but was defeated after landing on the south Caspian shores. His young son Ahmad became the new Shah, but the Majlis was now the real ruler of Iran. The early cabinets were neither experienced nor very successful, for the country was in a catastrophic economic state, and law and order were conspicuously absent.

To help solve the economic difficulties the Persian government in 1911 hired an American financial advisor, W. Morgan Shuster, who was a U.S. Treasury Department official but who came to Iran in a private capacity. Shuster organized a treasury gendarmerie to collect taxes and hoped to make various reforms, but he aroused the antagonism of the Russians, who demanded his ouster. At first the Majlis refused, but Russian troops began to march from Tabriz on Tehran so the Persian government capitulated and sent Shuster home.

It is difficult to realize the strong position of the Russians in Iran before World War I; it was a virtual military control of the northern part of the country. And it is not easy for the Persians to forget that when the people of Tabriz attacked Russian troops in protest against Russian action in the Shuster affair, the Russians not only repulsed the mob but in reprisal publicly hanged several of the leading citizens. In Meshed in the following year Russian troops bombarded the holy shrine of Imam Reza under the pretext that anti-foreign Persians were gathering there. This bombardment shocked the Muslim world, and even today it is an important factor in Persian distrust and fear of the Russians.

SOUTHERN OIL

In 1901 an Australian called William Knox D'Arcy obtained a concession from the Persian government for the exploitation of oil resources in all of Iran except the northern provinces. After much disappointment, a paying well was found in 1907 and operations began. In 1909 the Anglo-Persian Oil Co. was created, pipe lines were laid, and a refinery was constructed on the island of Abadan. Shortly before the war, when the Royal Navy changed to oil-burning ships, the British government invested a large sum in the company. Throughout the rest of the history of the company the British government has held a majority of its stock.

In the early years operations were very limited because of physical difficulties of work and transport, but steady progress has resulted in the largest refinery in the world at Abadan and complex drilling and pumping installations. Until the reign of Reza Shah the company paid the stipulated royalties to Tehran and also paid the local Bakhtiyari chiefs to guard the wells and protect the workers. Under Reza Shah the company began to expand its activities into education, health, and a host of services, but profits, of course, had grown tremendously. Oil became the prime source of revenue of the Iranian government and many felt the country should receive more royalties, but this belongs to a later story.

WORLD WAR I

The Persians were generally pro-German, since Germany was an enemy of their traditional foes, and German businessmen and products had made a good impression on the Persians. Iran remained neutral throughout the war despite the fact that battles were waged on her territory. Iran had only two military forces, both small; one was the Cossack brigade with Russian officers, while the other was a gendarmerie with Swedish officers. The Central Powers hoped to bring Persia into the war on their side and they almost succeeded.

The Germans sent some able agents to Iran to organize resistance to the Allies; perhaps the most famous was the former German consul Wassmus, who, disguised as a Persian, led the Qashqai tribes in fighting the British in Fars province. A pro-German government was organized in Kirmanshah near the Turkish frontier, but Turkish-German difficulties in Mesopotamia prevented them from helping their Persian friends effectively.

To counter German activities the British organized a military force of British, Indians, and Persians with British officers called the South Persia Rifles. By 1917 they had cleared southern Iran of German agents and had defeated quite a number of robber chieftains. The oil fields, of course, were guarded by British troops from an early stage of the war.

In the north the Russians had retreated before initial Turkish thrusts in the Caucasus region, but the Transcaucasian army, of which the Russian forces in Iran were a part, proved too strong for the Turks. In the spring of 1916 the Tsarist army penetrated deep into Turkey, capturing Erzerum, the largest Turkish military base in eastern Anatolia, while further to the south the Russians advanced towards Baghdad. At the end of April, however, a British army surrendered to the Turks at Kut al-Amara in Mesopotamia, thus releasing Turkish and German forces to attack the Russians in Iran. The Turks thereupon captured Hamadan and were advancing on Qazvin when winter stopped further operations.

The new year 1917 opened with British victories in Mesopotamia and Russian advances in Iran, but the revolution in Russia put an end to the victory march against the Turks. The disintegration of Russian forces in Iran in the summer of 1917 was swift, and only the weakness of the Ottoman army kept the Turks from immediately advancing into Iranian Azerbaijan. By the end of 1917 the military situation in northern Iran and the Caucasus had changed in favor of the Central Powers, and the Turks moved into Azerbaijan, defeating weak Armenian forces which had taken the place of the retreating Russians. This necessitated a counter move on the part of the British, who moved troops northeast of Tehran to defend the capital against a possible Turkish advance. There they remained until after the Armistice.

In southern Iran the Qashqai tribes, heartened by the great German offensive in northern France in the spring of 1918, revolted and attacked the British and Indian troops, at the same time inciting Persians to desert the South Persia Rifles. Much fighting was necessary before they were defeated and order was restored. By 1917 most of the German agents had been captured—only a few escaped to Turkey—and the worse was over for Iran. Numerous robber bands roamed at will over the countryside, however, and to this day in many hamlets of Iran those bandit chiefs are remembered with fear. The Bolshevik revolution in Russia had an important reaction in Iran, and the latter's troubles were not over with the signing of the Armistice.

THE SOVIETS AND BRITAIN

One of the first acts of the new Bolshevik government in regard to Iran was the renunciation of the 1907 Agreement with Great Britain. This created a favorable impression among the Persians, who now looked to the British to follow suit and evacuate their country. But the Soviets had not abandoned Iran; in May 1920 a Bolshevik flotilla followed the retreating remnants of the White forces of General Denikin into the Caspian ports of Iran. Here they joined forces with a bandit called Kuchik Khan, leader of a small army of "Jangalis," people of Gilan and Mazanderan. A

Soviet Republic of Gilan was proclaimed, a forerunner of the Azerbaijan republic of 1945. The Persian government, of course, protested, but the Soviets evaded the issue by claiming that this expedition was the action of the Azerbaijan Soviet republic and not of Moscow. Moscow, however, protested against the presence of British troops in Iran.

On February 26 of 1921 the Irano-Soviet treaty was concluded, and this treaty has remained the basis of Soviet-Iranian relations to the present time in spite of Iranian protests after World War II that membership in the United Nations made the treaty unnecessary. By the treaty Soviet Russia renounced all of the privileges of the Tsarist government in Iran, including the capitulations, and all concessions and property. It was an impressive gesture which pleased the Persians and raised Russian prestige in Iran. Fishing on the south Caspian shores was to be exploited by a joint company which in time came to be dominated by the Russians. Furthermore, Article 6 of the treaty gave the Soviets the right to send forces into Iran if the country should ever become a base for anti-Soviet activity. This clause provided the legal basis for the invasion of Iran by Soviet troops in 1941 and presumably still could be invoked if the Russians saw fit.

Since Articles 5 and 6 were and are so important, they are reproduced. Article 5 stated that the two governments undertake:

(1) To prohibit the formation or presence within their respective territories of any organization or group of persons, irrespective of the name by which they are known, whose object is to engage in acts of hostility against Persia or Russia, or against the Allies of Russia.

They will likewise prohibit the formation of armed troops within their respective territories with the aforementioned object.

(2) Not to allow a third Party or organization, whatever it be called, which is hostile to the other Contracting Party, to import or to convey in transit across their countries material which can be used against the other Party.

(3) To prevent by all means in their power the presence within

their territories or within the territories of their Allies of all armies or forces of a third Party in cases in which the presence of such forces would be regarded as a menace to the frontiers, interests or safety of the other Contracting Party.

Article 6 provides:

If a third Party should attempt to carry out a policy of usurpation by means of armed intervention in Persia, or if such Power should desire to use Persian territory as a base of operations against Russia, or if a Foreign Power should threaten the frontiers of Federal Russia or those of its Allies, and if the Persian Government should not be able to put a stop to such menace after having been once called upon to do so by Russia, Russia shall have the right to advance her troops into the Persian interior for the purpose of carrying out the military operations necessary for its defense. Russia undertakes, however, to withdraw her troops from Persian territory as soon as the danger has been removed.[2]

The British endeavored to conclude a much more comprehensive treaty with Iran in 1919. This agreement provided for British advisors in the economic and military fields, the sale of arms to a uniform Persian military force which the British would aid in organizing, and a loan to Iran. The agreement was kept a secret for some time, and when it was announced by the prime minister of Iran there was a storm of protest. Some Persians argued that it imposed a British protectorate on Iran and the agreement was discussed unfavorably in the press of Paris and Washington. Although Ahmad Shah finally supported the agreement, the Majlis had to ratify it, and it was necessary first to elect and convoke the National Assembly. This never happened because in February 1921 a new government came to power by a *coup d'état* which was to change the situation completely.

REZA SHAH PAHLEVI

Reza was an officer in the Persian Cossack brigade, and when the White Russian officers were dismissed on the pres-

[2] Text taken from N. S. Fatemi, *Diplomatic History of Persia, 1917-1923* (New York, 1952), 318-19.

sure of the British, he became the commander of the Cossacks. Together with a politician named Zia al-Din Tabatabai, he seized power by marching his troops to Tehran. Zia al-Din became prime minister, while Reza was minister of war and commander-in-chief of all Persian forces. The new government denounced the Anglo-Persian agreement, and it never came into effect. Later in 1921 Reza forced Zia al-Din to flee, and the British gave him asylum in Palestine. In 1923 Reza became prime minister and engineered the abdication of Ahmad Shah, who was in Europe. After considering the possibility of a republic, he mounted the peacock throne on December 17, 1925, and was crowned Reza Shah the following year.

British and Soviet troops had evacuated Iran by the end of 1921 and the first years of the new government were occupied with uniting the country. In order to accomplish this, the first task was to create an army and police force which would be loyal to the central government. After the defeat of Kuchik Khan, Kurdish rebels and the powerful chief of the Arabs in Khuzistan were subdued, and Iran was made more tranquil and united than at any time since the days of Shah 'Abbas. A gendarmerie in blue uniforms was created as well as an army; both were under the Ministry of War. The task of the gendarmerie was to maintain internal order, prevent smuggling, and to help in the collection of taxes. All over the country blockhouses were built where the gendarmes maintained a constant watch on the roads and also helped travellers in need.

Up to World War II the history of Iran is the story of Reza Shah, who took the family name Pahlevi, and his reforms. He undoubtedly took much of his inspiration from Mustafa Kemal Atatürk of Turkey, but he had a much more difficult task, for the Persians were not as prepared as the Turks for Westernization, since the Turks were closer to Europe and had been under Western influences much longer. Furthermore, Reza Shah had an individualistic people composed of many minorities and not so united as the Turks. He accomplished much in spite of opposition, yet it must be remembered that he was not always wise in his policies, and his tyranny and even cruelty at the end of his reign did much harm to Iran. After his abdication it was difficult to find capable young leaders to direct the destinies of the country, and graybeards from the pre-Reza Shah time, who could hardly be called liberals, had to lead the country.

Reza Shah's foreign policy was directed towards maintaining the freedom and integrity of Iran's frontiers. To further this he wanted friendly neighbors, and this prompted his visit to Ankara in 1934 to confer with Mustafa Kemal; this was the only time the Shah left his native land. Boundary disputes with Iraq and Afghanistan were settled amicably and on the 8th of July, 1937, a non-aggression and consultation pact was concluded between Iran, Iraq, Turkey, and Afghanistan. It was signed at the summer palace of the Shah north of Tehran and was known as the Sa'dabad Pact, after the name of the garden and palace.

The only other important diplomatic incident in Reza Shah's reign was the conflict with the Anglo-Iranian Oil Company. (In March, 1935, the Shah requested all foreign missions not to use the word Persia but the native word Iran for the country, and the Oil Company complied, along with the others. This order was later rescinded by the present Shah.) The company had grown enormously since World War I, but in 1932, because of the devaluation of the pound and the fall of oil prices on the world market, royalties paid to the Iranian government fell. Consequently Reza Shah declared the concession abrogated, maintaining that it had been secured when Iran had no representative government, an argument to be used in 1951 concerning Reza Shah's agreement. England brought the dispute to the League of Nations, but before any action was necessary Reza Shah's need for money and the desire of both sides to compromise brought a new agreement. The new concession was more limited in area than the old one; higher royalties were to be paid to Iran and more Persians were to be employed and trained by the company.

It is impossible here to discuss all of the reforms which Reza Shah initiated in his country. He abolished the remaining capitulations and instituted new civil and criminal codes based on the French codes, in spite of the opposition of the religious leaders. His other accomplishments may be divided into economic and social, with the latter perhaps the most significant and the most lasting.

Under the Qajars taxation had been almost on a personal basis, for rights of collection were farmed out to favorites or to the highest bidder. Reza Shah brought an American economic mission to Iran headed by Dr. A. C. Millspaugh, who remained in the country from 1922 to 1927. Millspaugh recommended the creation of state monopolies and other devices for raising money in the country without recourse to foreign loans, which had been so disastrous under the Qajars. Reza Shah cooperated with the mission until a clash of personalities led Millspaugh to leave. Germans replaced the American economic mission.

In 1927 a National Bank was founded which alone was granted the right to issue currency, formerly issued by the Imperial Bank, a British undertaking. The currency was also reformed, and a new unit, the *rial*, was created. Branches of the National Bank as well as other banks were established in provincial centers, and the economic life of the nation began to grow.

Transportation is extremely important in a mountainous land such as Iran, and Reza Shah realized that good roads were a necessity for the unification of the country and for economic growth. The most spectacular achievement in this domain was the trans-Iranian railroad. The revenues from the government tea and sugar monopolies were put aside for the cost of the railroad, and since tea is the national drink, used with copious quantities of sugar, the taxes were hardly popular; but they raised large sums towards the construction of the line. There is no question that the building of the railroad was one of the great engineering feats of modern times, for it traverses some of the most difficult terrain found on the globe. From Bandar-i-Shapur, the Prince's harbor on the Persian Gulf, to the plateau, it goes over the plain of Khuzistan, but then the line enters tortuous mountain ranges where the train is in the blackness of tunnels more than in the open sky. With over 150 tunnels on the southern line from Tehran to the Persian Gulf and half as many again on the northern line from Tehran to Bandar-i-Shah on the Caspian, the trans-Iranian railroad was a very costly enterprise. It was completed shortly before the last war; and to Reza Shah, who planned that it would approach neither the Russian system in the Caucasus nor the British lines in Iraq or Baluchistan, it must have seemed an irony of history that it should have proved so helpful to his enemies during the war.

While Reza Shah did not neglect agriculture, the backbone of the nation's economy, he hoped to make his country independent of many foreign goods by building factories. Nine sugar factories were erected; factories for matches, spinning and weaving, glass, and many others were built in various parts of the country. In most of them the government took an active part in providing capital and training workers, for private enterprise was and remains embryonic. The metric system of weights and measures was introduced in place of many local measures. In trade the state controlled all exports and imports. To all intents and purposes Iran had become a national socialist state by 1941, a fact which was reflected also in the social reforms instituted by fiat.

Under Reza Shah there was no unemployment and a proletariat had not developed, so social reforms mainly were directed towards the emancipation of women and the eradication of many traditional but backward practices sanctioned by religion. Persian women used to wear thick black veils, but in 1936, after a lengthy preparation, women were ordered to take off their veils. Policemen were ordered to remove their veils on the streets, and this, of course, led to the wearing of European dresses. Girls' schools were built, girl scout groups organized, and women were encouraged to take a part in the social and economic life of the country. This was a tremendous change in a country where women previously had no public existence. At the same time men had to wear

European costume and hats. At first Reza Shah introduced a "Pahlevi cap," like a French *kepi,* but later any European headgear was permitted. All of this, while it sometimes led to opposition from conservative men or women, was necessary to change Iran from an Oriental to a Western nation; for the neighboring Turkish leader had demonstrated well the great importance of change from a fez to a Western hat in the minds of the Turks.

There was also what might be termed a cultural revival under Reza Shah following a decline under the Qajars. Native crafts—tilework, carpets with plant dye colors, brass work, and others—had declined before foreign mass production, but the new Shah sought to revive them by establishing art schools and fostering craftsmen. In architecture a neo-Achaemenid or neo-Sassanian style was used extensively—for example, in the National Bank building, the Police offices, and the archaeology museum in Tehran. A new Islamic style of architecture with profuse tile work was also developed and used in buildings such as the new mausoleums of Sa'di and Hafiz in Shiraz. Other arts too were fostered and developed.

Reza Shah realized that the youth of the country, in whom the future lay, needed education, so large sums were spent on schools, and in 1935 the University of Tehran was founded. Hundreds of advanced students were sent to Europe for further training, mainly in science and medicine. In the same year as the founding of the University, an Iranian Academy was founded on the model of the French Academy with the prime purpose to study and renovate the Persian language. Attempts to purge Persian of its Arabic words were not too successful, but there was a new interest in reforms of Persian poetry and literature as more European literary works were translated into Persian.

Reza Shah had the most opposition from the *mullahs* and religiously conservative people, for they realized that his success meant a loss in their hold on the populace. In tests of strength Reza Shah won, even by using machine guns in the holy shrine at Meshed. He opened the mosques to foreign tourists, thus flouting the religious leaders, many of whom thought it wise to flee from Iran as long as Reza Shah was alive.

The innovations of Reza Shah are legion, but sometimes he tried too much. A music school was created, and Tehran was to have an opera. The opera house still stands an empty shell in the heart of the capital, never having been completed. The press was effectively muzzled by the government, and the movement of people in the country, especially foreigners, was controlled by the gendarmes.

The Shah had never been noted for his friendliness or kindness, and after he removed his able prime minister and friend, Timurtash, and had him killed in 1933, he became more morose and brutal. Likewise his greed knew no bounds, and he seized estates which pleased him until he had vast land holdings in Mazanderan. To obtain more money for the rice from his estates he forebade the growing of rice elsewhere in the country—in Seistan, Baluchistan, and Khuzistan. His people trembled when their ruler passed in his limousine, for he inspired fear in all of his subjects.

WORLD WAR II

Reza Shah was suspicious of the Russians and British, so it was only natural that he would turn to Germany for technical advisors. With the advent of Hitler, Germany showed a new interest in Iran, and technicians, doctors, and various advisors were sent on terms usually favorable to Iran. Trade between the two countries developed apace so that Germany was receiving 41 per cent of Iran's foreign trade at the outbreak of war.

Iran proclaimed her neutrality, though many Persians were undoubtedly pro-German. There was no cause for quarrel with the Russians or British until the Nazi invasion of the Soviet Union in June, 1941. It should have been apparent to Reza Shah that Iran was the only feasible road for the shipment of war supplies to Russia; the northern sea route to Murmansk would be under enemy attack while

Vladivostok was too far away. The two great powers asked the Iranian government for permission to use Iran as a route of transport shortly after the Nazi attack on the USSR. Reza Shah refused and in August received an ultimatum. When he again refused, Soviet and British forces moved into the country. In the south the British had some opposition, but the Red Army in the north met no resistance. The country was divided into a northern zone—including the Caspian provinces plus Azerbaijan and Khurasan—occupied by Soviet troops and a southern zone—the rest of the country—under the British. Reza Shah abdicated under Allied pressure and his son Muhammad (Mohammed) Reza, the present ruler, took his place. Reza Shah was taken to South Africa, where he died in 1944.

The occupation of Iran brought an abrupt change in her history; it was the end of the era of accelerated reforms under the goading of a strong ruler. Many Persians, and undoubtedly Reza Shah himself, had illusions about the strength of the country and the progress it had made. The occupation and abdication of the sole authority in the land left the Persian people bewildered and unable to act for themselves. No one had held authority under Reza Shah, and now democratic political parties were to be formed to occupy the vacuum left by the dictator's fall.

Britain and the Soviet Union formalized their occupation of the country by a Tripartite Treaty of Alliance on January 29, 1942, which must have sounded familiar to old Persian ears. The treaty, as usual, guaranteed the integrity and independence of Iran and stated that there was to be no "occupation," rather the three governments were helping each other in a common end—the defeat of the Nazis. It also provided for the withdrawal of Allied troops within six months after the end of the war with the Axis. With the occupation, inflation began to plague the Persians following the breakdown of transportation and order in the country. Communists and other political prisoners were released from jail and immediately began to organize political groups. Thus was born the Tudeh or "Masses" party, the Communist party of Iran.

The Soviets aided this party by money and even by military support in their zone of occupation. Persian soldiers who had been taken prisoner to Soviet Central Asia were indoctrinated with Communist propaganda and released to return home singing Soviet praises. The Iranian government was unable to operate freely, since Soviet troops usually refused to permit government officials to enter the northern part of their own country. The British imposed no restrictions and, in fact, greatly aided the Iranian government by establishing a transport company called the United Kingdom Commercial Corporation to carry grain and supplies for the Persians as well as war supplies for the Russians.

The American Persian Gulf Command, first a service section of the Middle East Command, had about 30,000 soldiers, mainly transport troops, in Iran from 1942 to 1945. They came to Iran to aid the British in sending supplies to Russia, and their commanding general took special pains not to offend the Russians, even ordering his own intelligence unit to depart at the request of the Red Army. The United States not only knew little about Iranian affairs but showed little interest in their development during the war. It is true that the presence of American troops kindled some interest and activity in the USA and the short-lived economic mission headed by Millspaugh in 1943-44 to help the Persians had more official American recognition than any previous group. Nonetheless there was a real lack of awareness of the political problems of the day and the possible shape of things to come in Iran on the part of the Americans on the scene.

The Persians turned to the United States for other help; lend-lease was granted to Iran; a military mission was sent to advise the Persian army, and an American Colonel Schwartzkopf, was sent to reorganize the gendarmerie. These and other advisors in health, education, and the like could not but annoy the Soviets, who regarded a new power on the scene in Iran as a possible source of trouble for future Russian plans.

On December 1, 1943, the Tehran Declaration was issued

by the Big Three, reaffirming the Atlantic Charter, re-emphasizing the integrity and independence of Iran, and promising her economic aid during and after the war. This greatly heartened the Persians, who suspected from the tone of the Declaration that it had been Roosevelt's idea.[3] Red Army troops in Iran received orders to be more friendly to the British and Americans rather than to complain of the absence of a second front, and relations improved for a short time.

As the war receded and the danger of an Axis advance from the Caucasus vanished, the fear of a fifth-column movement in Iran subsided. German agents who had parachuted into the country in the spring of 1943 were captured, and pro-Axis Iranians were arrested several months later, shortly before Iran declared war on Germany on September 9, 1943. The new world situation caused a change of Russian attitude in the country. Heretofore the Russians had been occupied with saving themselves; now they took an interest in internal Persian politics with a view to furthering their own ends.

In the elections to the new Majlis, finally completed in the spring of 1944, the Tudeh party won 8 seats out of 130. The Communists represented the only organized party; other groups in parliament supported various popular leaders. This is not to say that political groups did not exist outside the Majlis—the most important was a pro-British organization headed by Zia al-Din Tabatabai, who had returned from exile after the abdication of Reza Shah—but there were no real parties in the European sense with programs and members in the Majlis. This somewhat chaotic state of Iranian politics worked to the advantage of the Communists, who had a clear purpose and disciplined followers while the opposition was disunited.

The Soviet embassy sponsored propaganda libraries, cultural exchanges, journals, and motion pictures throughout the country. The minorities, especially the Armenians, were wooed by Soviet favors, and after the war many Armenians migrated from Iran to the Soviet Union. The

[3] See Appendix III.

Russians also participated in the Anglo-Soviet-Iranian censorship imposed on the country, but they took care that they always had the best of the bargain.[4] In general, the tenor of Soviet propaganda in Iran during the war was to extol life in the Soviet Union and to stress the power of the Red Army as the sole conquerors of the Nazi armies. Towards the end this changed.

The turning point in Soviet relations with Iran came in September, 1944, when Kavtaradze, a vice-commissar for Foreign Affairs, arrived from Moscow to negotiate an agreement for the exploitation of oil in northern Iran. Earlier in the same year American and British oil companies had evinced an interest in obtaining concessions outside of the Anglo-Iranian Oil Company's domain. After many rumors had spread in the bazaars, the Iranian government announced on October 16 that no concessions would be granted. This created a storm of protest and vituperation against the government from the Tudeh press, and mass meetings were held by the Communists to urge their government to grant a concession to the USSR. In spite of the pressure from the Soviets and the Tudeh followers, on December 2, 1944, the Majlis passed a law, proposed by Dr. Mossadegh, that no cabinet minister could enter into negotiation or grant oil concessions to foreigners without the approval of the Majlis. Kavtaradze left Iran saying that the law was a great mistake and Irano-Soviet relations would thereby suffer. It was after this rebuff on the oil concession that the Soviets and their minions adopted a more anti-Western line, for the Americans, and especially the British, were accused of supporting the reactionary Iranian government. Vituperation that was formerly anti-Nazi was now shifted against Russia's allies.

By January, 1945, Iran had ceased to be important for the shipment of war supplies, so the Persians sought the evacuation of foreign troops from their country. Legally, the Soviets maintained, troops could be retained six months after the end of the war with the Axis, which included

[4] Cf. G. Lenczowski, *Russia and the West in Iran, 1918-1948* (Cornell, 1949), 206.

Japan. American troops withdrew before the end of the year while gradually the British, and reluctantly the Russians, disbanded their various organizations in Tehran. By the time of the Japanese surrender, however, a new problem had appeared which was to occupy the headlines of the press throughout the world.

THE AZERBAIJAN REPUBLIC

In August, 1945, the Tudeh party took over several government buildings in Tabriz and published leaflets seeking autonomy for Azerbaijan, the official use of the Azeri Turkish language, and a reform of the provincial economy. Red Army troops prevented Persian forces from marching to Tabriz to quell the uprising. The rebels could have taken control at that time, but apparently the Soviet Union was not quite ready to show its hand. The Tudeh party in Azerbaijan was renovated and renamed the Democratic party, which began anew to press demands for autonomy. All took place under the protection of Soviet troops, who continued to refuse to allow central government forces in the province. By November the Democrats were in complete control and on December 12 the newly elected assembly in Tabriz proclaimed the Autonomous Republic of Azerbaijan. A Communist agent who had spent many years in the USSR, Ja'far Pishevari, became the prime minister. A "people's army," supplied by the Russians, was formed and a police state began to operate.

In addition to the Azerbaijan republic, a Kurdish republic was set up with its capital at Mahabad, but it was less significant than the state created by their neighbors, nor did it receive as much material aid from the Russians. A treaty of alliance was signed between the two rebel governments, but the Kurdish state gained little if anything by it. Soviet agents were very active in both governments, since there were both Kurds and Azerbaijanis living in the USSR and it was easy to cross the frontier. It is interesting to note that the publications by the rebels in Azeri Turkish revealed their Russian origin, for words were used that are not current in Iranian Azerbaijan.

The Azerbaijan crisis before the United Nations is recent history. This was the first major instance of Soviet obstruction which the new world assembly encountered. Iran complained to the United Nations of the interference of Soviet Russia in her internal affairs, and the Western powers linked the Azerbaijan crisis with the unwillingness of the Red Army to evacuate Iran. At the conference of Foreign Ministers of the three great powers in Moscow in December, 1945, no agreement had been reached on the evacuation of Iran and on a committee of investigation for Azerbaijan. The Security Council, after much heated debate, decided to refer the matter to Iran and the USSR for direct negotiation.

A new prime minister, Ahmad Qavam (Ghavam al-Saltaneh), went to Moscow in February, 1946, to make an agreement with the Russians, but when March 2 passed and Soviet troops remained on Persian soil, he protested and returned to Tehran. Once the USSR had broken the 1942 treaty to evacuate her troops from Iran within six months after the end of the war with the Axis, the Russians were open to attack in the United Nations and by world opinion. In order to secure the withdrawal of the Red Army, Qavam made three concessions to the Russians. He agreed to the establishment of a Soviet-Iranian company to exploit the oil resources of northern Iran—the Soviets to hold 51% of the stock; he further instructed Iran's delegate at the UN to withdraw Iran's complaint against the Soviet Union (which the delegate refused to do); and finally he gave the Tudeh party three places in his cabinet. Qavam also promised to enter into negotiations with the Democrats in Azerbaijan to guarantee their rights and to recognize them as the legal provincial government. As a result, the Red Army finally evacuated Iran on May 9, 1946, but the Soviet Union seemed to remain the victor in the affair.

A new Majlis had to be elected to approve the agreements made by Qavam with the Soviets, but with Tudeh members in Qavam's cabinet and agents active in the country, it seemed as though Iran was destined to fall on Russia's side of the fence. Riots in the oil fields and Abadan were instigated by Tudeh agents, and the riots brought an increase in British forces in nearby Basra. But it was the tribal revolt in the south, led by the Qashqais, which saved the day for the West. The tribal chiefs demanded that Qavam dismiss the Communists from his cabinet, which he did on October 17. Next came the question of elections, and Qavam insisted that the central government would have to supervise elections even in Azerbaijan. The Russians were in a dilemma as to which to support, the Azerbaijan Democrats, or Qavam, who had promised them oil. Qavam ordered troops into the province, and the rebel government collapsed when Tabriz was lost on December 15, 1946. Tudeh followers all over Iran were arrested, and the Kurdish republic came to an end shortly after the fall of the Azerbaijan republic.

The Soviet Union still hoped to maintain its influence by the ratification of the oil agreement, but the new (fifteenth) parliament, inaugurated in the middle of August, was in no hurry to ratify it. The new American ambassador, George V. Allen, stiffened Persian resistance to the accord by declaring American support of Persian freedom to accept or reject the agreement on its merits and value to Iran. On October 22, 1947, the Majlis rejected Qavam's oil agreement. Iran was lost to the Soviet Union and at once became a target of Communist intrigues and an arena for the ever-growing anti-American propaganda campaign.

GROWING AMERICAN INFLUENCE

Americans, in private capacity, had created over the years a legacy of good will among the Persians. Missionaries had constructed hospitals and schools in northern Iran which served the Persian people for decades, and the prestige of Americans in Iran had been greatly enhanced by such individuals as the economic advisor Morgan Shuster and Dr. Jordan, for many years head of Alburz College, which was taken over by Reza Shah from the Americans shortly before the last war. The post-war period saw a great growth of official American activity in Iran. The military missions to the army and gendarmerie were continued after the war; military supplies were sent to Iran in 1949 and credits were extended for the purchase of such equipment. The engineering firm of Morris-Knudsen was employed in 1947 to prepare an extensive survey for the economic development of Iran. As a result a Seven Year Plan was approved by the Majlis on February 15, 1949, and American advisors, belonging to Overseas Consultants, Inc., were hired to put the plan into operation. This tremendous expansion of Iran's industry, agriculture, schools, etc., required an expenditure of $650,-000,000, most of which was to be obtained from oil royalties. Additional loans, however, were necessary, and this was the prime reason for the Shah's trip to the United States in the autumn of 1949.

The Shah was well received and his visit was a personal success, but he got no loans. Instead, promises of Point Four and military aid, as well as support for an Iranian request for a sizable loan from the World Bank, were given him. The Shah was admonished that Iran had to clean its own house of inefficiency and corruption before the confidence of any bankers could be won. Upon his return this is what the Shah sought to do. He turned over the royal estates to a newly created organization for social welfare and in June, 1950, appointed General 'Ali Razmara his reformer prime minister. The future looked bright, and the new American ambassador, among others, was obviously pleased by the direction taken by the new government.

Razmara proposed a revision of the administrative organization of the country, creating village councils and decentralizing government control. Numerous officials were dismissed on the grounds of corruption or incompetence, and other officials were put on their best behavior. This activity was carried out partially to convince the United States that Iran was really cleaning house in preparation for a large loan.

When the Export-Import Bank announced it would loan the Persian government only $25,000,000, the Persians were extremely disappointed. Neither the American government nor the World Bank had offered any loans to Iran, and the Point Four grant of half a million dollars was inadequate. The Shah was outspoken in his criticism, and there were bitter words in the Majlis about America. The Seven Year Plan was in danger and the American experts with Overseas Consultants left Iran in January, 1951, when their contracts were not renewed. Razmara was also bitter and prohibited the Voice of America relay over radio Tehran, as well as BBC broadcasts. Then he concluded a trade agreement with Soviet Russia for $20,000,000, which indicated that Iran would deal with her northern neighbor if it were to her advantage. While American prestige suffered as a result of the failure of large loans to materialize, there was more disappointment than turning from the Americans to Russia.

Razmara was an energetic soldier who had the confidence of the Shah but not of the Majlis. He had led the Persian troops against the Azerbaijan rebels and was popular in the army, but his plans for reform met opposition among the wealthy landlords as well as from the extreme left. Nonetheless, the prime minister was resolved to put his reforms into operation in the face of opposition from the Majlis. The Senate, which had come into existence in 1948, and half of whose members were appointed by the Shah, was more responsive to the attempts of Razmara to reform the government and economy of the country. Iran was in great need of reform, for taxes had fallen, due partially to the poor harvests of 1948 and 1949 but also to the prevalent unrest and lack of confidence in the government. Several revolts in Kurdistan were ended only with difficulty, and the ugly phenomenon of political assassination appeared. A journalist and a court minister were shot, while on February 4, 1949, there was an attempt on the life of the Shah, which wounded him only slightly. This for a time roused the public against acts of terrorism; but what was the temper of the people before the assassination of Razmara, and what were the hidden elements behind it?

One must remember that the tradition of secret societies

is both old and popular in Iran. The relatively innocuous dervish orders have been mentioned, but they are supported by older intellectuals and businessmen. Ever since the fall of Reza Shah the religious leaders had been seeking to regain the power which they lost under his regime. With little publicity the *mullahs* had been working in the countryside to secure support for an Islamic revival, which also meant a return of their power. Nor did their appeals fall on deaf ears, for many Persians thought they had been pushed too fast towards secularism and Westernization. The alleged leader of one group of reactionary fanatics, the *Fadayan-i-Islam,* was Ayatollah Kashani, an elderly religious leader who was high in popular esteem. He had once been exiled from Iran, but his external connection if anything helped him in his work at home. The *Fadayan* had roughly the same goals as the Muslim Brotherhood in Egypt—a regenerated Islam and a willingness to sacrifice one's life if necessary for God and country, for the *Fadayan* are extreme nationalists as well as religious fanatics.

Kashani and his followers are anti-Communist, maintaining that Islam is incompatible with Communism; but they were willing to unite for a short time with the Tudeh in anti-British demonstrations in 1952. The aim of Kashani is to influence the government from behind the scenes while working for the restoration of privileges and power to the religious leaders. On a large scale he hopes for a pan-Islamic revival, but that is far in the future.

Communism had made its greatest inroads among the youth, and university students were the most voluble supporters of the Tudeh by their participation in strikes and riots in Tehran. Disillusioned white-collar workers, rather than the small proletariat, provided the second mainstay of the Tudeh, while the peasantry on the whole was apathetic. Several prominent literary figures wrote pro-Communist essays or poems, more in protest against the discouraging situation in Iran than with any real understanding of the meaning of Marxism or the Stalinism of the Soviet Union.

The vast mass of the people, on the other hand, were comparatively unaffected by ideologies, but they reacted strongly to pressure on their stomachs. Most of them, living on the margin of starvation, would be immediately concerned if the harvest were bad or if prices rose. With the beginning of the Korean war prices began to climb in Iran, and Persians remembered war days when Tehran was second only to Chungking in the size of its inflation. Beggars increased on the streets of Tehran, and Razmara's attempts to rehabilitate them in special villages near the capital were not successful owing to their ever-growing numbers. So discontent was rife among all classes.

The government was in sore straits and needed money to carry out reforms as well as to keep up with a swelling bureaucracy. Furthermore there was an endeavor to continue as much of the Seven Year Plan as was possible with available funds. A national oil company was created under this plan to explore and exploit oil in areas outside the Anglo-Iranian concession, but it required large sums to continue its work. The only obvious source of more revenue was the Anglo-Iranian Oil Company, and Persians now turned their attention to oil.

OIL: THE LIFE BLOOD OF IRANIAN ECONOMY

While the Iranian government continued to receive an increasing amount of royalties from the AIOC, profits for the company had developed apace. With expanding operations came a larger plant, more employees, and extended services. In the words of the British Commercial Counsellor in Tehran:[5]

The vast development of the Oil Company's activities has entailed a heavy responsibility and a heavy task in maintaining a corresponding development in the housing, health and social welfare of the Company's staff of 66,000, who, with their families and dependents, make up a scattered community of nearly

[5] N. S. Roberts, *Iran, Overseas Economic Surveys* (London, 1948), 38.

200,000, representing some sixty trades and professions directly concerned in the oil industry.

And in the realm of health there were seventy full-time doctors and two fully equipped hospitals. In education, "the Company has built and equipped, and largely maintains, seventeen schools in Khuzistan with accommodation for 7,280 pupils. The Company this year [1948] has provided school accommodation for 3,672 of the 4,850 pupils attending schools in Abadan."[6]

Production in the oil fields rose from 8 million tons in 1940 to 17 million in 1945 and over 20 million in 1948.[7] But Persians claimed they were not receiving a just share of the profits; and when Dr. Mossadegh, leader of the bloc of deputies in the Majlis who wanted to nationalize the AIOC, produced figures on the expenses of the Oil Company, he gained added support from the populace for his nationalization program. Dr. Mossadegh claimed that in 1949 the AIOC had the following expenses (reported in the newspaper *Itala'at*):

British income tax	£28 million
Dividends to shareholders	£ 7 million
Royalties to Iran	£10 million
Reserves	£17 million
Operational Expenditures	£17 million
Total	£79 million

Events followed each other in rapid succession after Prime Minister Razmara declared on the floor of the Majlis that the Persians were incapable of operating the AIOC installations in Iran. Three days after he opposed the demands for nationalization of oil, he was shot to death in a Tehran mosque by a fanatic belonging to the *Fadayan-i-Islam*. The following day the Majlis oil committee voted unanimously to nationalize the AIOC, and one week later the Majlis approved the nationalization action also in a unanimous vote.

[6] *Ibid.*, 39.
[7] *Iran d'hier et d'aujourd'hui*, Ambassade de l'Iran (Paris, 1950), 43.

This was a signal for Communist as well as nationalist demonstrations and the beginning of the anti-British movement which grew to extremes in 1952.

The Russians reacted to the nationalization in a crude attempt to create rivalry between Britain and the United States by accusing the Americans of having engineered the assassination to help American oil companies in replacing the AIOC. Hopes of a compromise between Iran and the Company faded when strikes broke out in the oil fields, and in spite of martial law three British subjects were killed on April 12. The new prime minister, Hussein Ala, former ambassador to the United States, sought to reconcile the conflicting interests, but the Majlis was resolved to pass a law for the immediate seizure of the AIOC. Fanatics threatened the lives of him and his cabinet members, so he resigned on April 27. The next day the bill for full nationalization and seizure was passed by the Majlis, and Dr. Mossadegh became prime minister.

Dr. Mossadegh, the champion of nationalization, proved to be an astute politician, capable of various histrionics, but with a shrewd talent for enlisting popular support. He had shown his courage in 1944 when he proposed the law forbidding any minister to discuss oil concessions, while behind him the British and Soviet ambassadors almost breathed down his neck from the diplomats' gallery in the Majlis. His reputation for honesty gained him a high regard even from his opponents. But Mosadegh was not regarded as an expert on foreign policy, and to many outsiders it seemed as though he were a puppet of his more fanatic followers in his National Front bloc. In any case, shortly after the nationalization of oil an anti-British campaign started over radio Tehran, in the newspapers, and in numerous demonstrations and speeches in all parts of the country. Even in isolated villages, where no Englishman had set foot, they or their agents were blamed for various local ills. Politicians from all sides hastened to support the popular Dr. Mossadegh, using the British scapegoat as the reason for all the corruption and mismanagement of affairs in the past.

Among the Persians, however, were some discordant voices, primarily the Communists, who, at first unable to take advantage of the situation, began to censure Dr. Mossadegh as the tool of American capitalism. The Tudeh party, though officially outlawed since the attempt on the Shah's life, worked underground and on May 8, 1951, after a successful May Day demonstration in Tehran, sent an open letter to Dr. Mossadegh demanding that he expel the American military mission with the Persian army, legalize the Tudeh party, abolish martial law, and recognize Communist China. The prime minister refused to accede to their demands, but their open activities increased. The *Fadayan-i-Islam* also proved a recalcitrant group, pressing for quick action on implementation of the oil nationalization law and even supporting the Tudeh in some of their demands. So Dr. Mossadegh had complete support only for his oil nationalization program; the opposition was to increase in 1952 and provide difficult decisions for Mossadegh to make.

The United States government was greatly concerned over the oil crisis, and on June 1, 1951, President Truman sent messages to the British and Iranian governments urging them to settle the dispute to mutual advantage. On June 12 several directors of the AIOC arrived in Tehran for talks with the Persians, but the latter wanted immediate recognition of the nationalization which the British at that time were not prepared to concede. On June 22 the British oil delegation returned to London, while Great Britain requested the International Court of Justice in the Hague to issue an injunction to prevent Iran from seizing the Oil Company's property. The Persians, meanwhile, went ahead with their plans and sent receipts of the National Oil Company of Iran to the captains of the tankers loading oil at Abadan, whereupon the AIOC ordered the tankers to pump their oil back to the storage tanks on shore and to leave Abadan. When the International Court recommended that the AIOC be given its properties while revenues would be frozen in bank accounts, the Iranian government on July 9 sent a message to the UN to withdraw from the International Court. On July 15 W.

Averell Harriman arrived in Tehran to lend his good offices to a reconciliation, and shortly thereafter Richard Stokes, Lord Privy Seal, arrived from London to discuss the question on a government level. On August 13 he presented an eight-point plan for a solution of the oil crisis in which the British recognized nationalization and agreed to turn over the property of the AIOC in Iran to the National Oil Co. on certain conditions. These conditions centered around the creation of a Purchasing Organization, the primary function of which would be to arrange for the sale and transport of Iranian oil. The Persians suspected that this arrangement would maintain the British in control of their oil, and they rejected the proposal. This prompted an announcement by the AIOC that they would bring suit against anyone who bought oil from Abadan. On September 27 Iranian troops took over the refinery at Abadan, and on October 3 the last British technicians departed, leaving the Persians in complete control.

On the diplomatic front Great Britain brought the oil dispute before the United Nations, at first calling upon Iran to heed the recommendation of the International Court, but later changing to a request for negotiation. The Security Council requested the International Court to rule on the Council's competence to deal with the oil crisis. Dr. Mossadegh came to the United States in October, 1951, and spoke before the UN. Afterwards he conferred with American officials, but attempts at reconciliation with the British failed. The prime minister then requested a loan of $120 million from the United States to repair the choatic state of Iran's economy. On his return from the United States Mossadegh received a tremendous ovation in Tehran which strengthened him in his next move—the calling for national elections in spite of the decision of the Majlis to postpone the elections.

Throughout the winter the two most important items of news in Iran were the efforts of the International Bank to reach an agreement with the Iranian government and the elections. It seemed as though a satisfactory solution of the oil controversy could be reached by the agreement of the

Bank to finance and operate the oil industry. On January 3, 1952, Mossadegh rejected the Bank's proposals, insisting that the Bank would have to carry out the orders of the Iranian government. Further negotiations were planned, but in the face of Persian determination to hire no British personnel, and general hostility to the British, a compromise seemed difficult of achievement, as it later proved to be.

The elections were planned with care. Governors and gendarme and army officers were moved to other provinces so they could not influence the local elections, and the elections were staggered so that order could be better maintained. Nonetheless election riots caused the deaths of numerous Persians in the provincial towns. Even in far-off Zabul on the Afghan frontier the Christian chief of the Narui Baluchi tribe was killed in an election demonstration. In the new Majlis Dr. Mossadegh received additional support, but with the individualistic deputies he could not be sure of continued support.

In March, negotiations with the Bank on oil collapsed over the proposed authority of the Bank, its desire to use British technicians, and the price of oil. Mossadegh flew to the Hague in June and ably defended Iran's case before the International Court, pleading that the Court had no jurisdiction over a dispute between a company and the Iranian government. On his return from Europe the crowds who greeted him at the airport were much smaller and less enthusiastic than they had been the previous year when he returned from America. The time seemed propitious for a change, and when Mossadegh requested exceptional powers from the new Majlis, many members balked. Mossadegh resigned on July 5, but the Shah and the two houses of parliament tried to conciliate him. This only increased Mossadegh's demands; on July 13 he asked for full powers in the economic and banking fields, and two days later he declared he would be his own war minister with dictatorial power. This was too much, and the Shah appointed Ahmad Qavam to be the new prime minister.

For three days there were riots in the cities of Iran. In

Tehran the Communists joined the *Fadayan* and nationalist supporters of Mossadegh in wild demonstrations against Qavam. Many rioters and policemen were killed. Qavam, to preserve order, requested full powers to use the police and army to quell the disorders, but the Majlis refused to support him, so Qavam resigned July 21. The following day, triumphant Dr. Mossadegh, vindicated by the demonstrations in his favor, returned to power.

During the riots the Communists had raised their usual anti-American slogans, but a new move was their propaganda against the Shah. This latter misfired, for the nationalists turned against their Communist comrades for daring too much. It was indicative, however, of the steady progress of Communist plans, testing their strength here and there, consolidating where they could but retreating if necessary. As a consequence of the riots extremist elements came to the fore and many members of parliament were terrorized. Later in the year extremists succeeded in obtaining a pardon with honors for the assassin of Razmara, who became a hero instead of a criminal. They also succeeded in opening proceedings against Qavam for treason for his part in the riots of July. Mossadegh, to further consolidate his position, decided to reorganize the Supreme Court, which might have opposed some of his acts as unconstitutional. He likewise dissolved the Senate, although the six year terms of the senators had not expired.

On July 22 the International Court ruled that it did not have competence in the oil dispute, cancelling its year-old injunction to restore the oil property to the AIOC. Mossadegh won a victory thereby which strengthened his prestige at home but did nothing to solve the financial problems besetting Iran. But what of the oil fields and vast installations themselves?

Contrary to the predictions of the AIOC, Persian engineers were able to continue operations and the storage tanks were filled, but no customers came to buy. Because of the AIOC threat to sue purchasers of what they considered the company's oil, no tanker was willing to take a risk. In the spring of 1952 one tanker, the Rose Mary, attempted to carry oil to Italy but was seized at Aden. The Persians complained of a British blockade which was strangling their economy, based as it was on the oil revenues. In the long run, however, the most harm to Abadan would come from the expansion of oil activities in Kuwait, Iraq, and Saudi Arabia, where there was adequate crude oil to meet all demands. The refineries which were being built at Bombay, Basra, and elsewhere would soon offset the greatest asset of the Persians—the Abadan refinery. And, inasmuch as the oil business is highly competitive, new plants, new processes, and methods were sure to affect adversely the hopes of the Persians to regain lost ground. In the endurance contest between the Persians and the British victory seemed assured to the latter. Many Persians feared this, but for them the entire dispute was more emotional and political than economic, and many swore they would prefer to see Abadan destroyed rather than make a deal with the British. But they also knew the great powers of endurance of their own people. For the Persians it was a question of freedom from British imperialism, political as well as economic, rather than a question simply of the nationalization of an industry. This was made clear by the acts of the Iranian government in 1952: the expulsion of British newspaper correspondents; the closing of all British consulates in January; the ban on all foreign cultural institutions and information libraries outside of Tehran on February 5; and finally the breaking of diplomatic relations with Britain in October. It is difficult to describe the effect of the lowering of the Union Jack on October 22 from the flagpole of the huge walled British embassy in the heart of Tehran, the first time it had happened in modern Iran. A belated attempt to compromise on the oil question was made by Winston Churchill and President Truman in a joint note to Iran on August 27. Three proposals were made: the question of compensation to be submitted to the International Court; representatives of the AIOC and the Iranian government to negotiate for resumption of oil shipments from Abadan; and if the first two were accepted, Britain to relax restrictions on exports to Iran and on Iran's use of sterling, while the United States would grant Iran 10 million dollars at once to assist the Iranians in their budgetary problems. Mossadegh rejected the proposal and on September 24 made a counter proposal, the chief feature of which was the payment of 49 million pounds to Iran by the AIOC, due Iran in 1950 as increases in royalty, taxes, and dividends. On October 7, after an exchange of notes with Acheson and Eden, Mossadegh proposed the advance payment of 20 million pounds convertible into dollars by the Company as a condition to the re-opening of negotiations.[8] This was unacceptable to the AIOC and the matter rested.

FUTURE PROSPECTS

Since the United States has replaced Britain as the guardian of Western interests in Iran, a glance at American activity in the country is desirable. On the physical side the number of Americans attached to the Embassy increased considerably in 1951 and 1952, making Tehran one of the largest non-military American foreign posts. A large embassy compound with garages, dispensary, independent water supply, and other amenities was finished in 1952. In addition to embassy and military personnel, Point Four technicians arrived in Iran in the spring of summer of 1952 to implement the 23 million dollars which had been allotted Iran for 1952. The construction of wells and plans for irrigation projects made a favorable impression on the Persians and bodes well for the future if Point Four aid is continued. A great advance was made on September 17, 1952, when the Shah inaugurated the Bank for Rural Credit, a joint enterprise in which the Technical Cooperation Administration (Point Four) provides $500,000—half the initial capital to start the Bank. The purpose of the Bank will be to finance cooperatives and to aid in the training of farm supervisors. As the *Department of State Bulletin* says: "This marks the first major step by the United States to implement in the

[8] Texts of notes in *Middle Eastern Affairs* (October, 1942), 284-292.

Middle East its policy of cooperating with other governments in carrying out programs of land reform which they initiate themselves."[9]

In the military sphere the shipment of arms to Iran under the Mutual Security Act was halted in January 1952 because Iran failed to comply with the conditions of that Act, but on April 25, after conversations with Dr. Mossadegh, an agreement was made and the USA resumed military aid to Iran. This brought forth a strong protest from the Soviet Union to Iran that American military aid violated the Irano-Soviet Treaty of 1921, but the Persians rejected the Soviet protests and aid continued. The Russians kept up their attacks by press and radio on the reactionary government in Iran, while Soviet agents in Tehran organized anti-American demonstrations protesting germ warfare in Korea and American interference in Iran's internal affairs. Many Persians were puzzled that the Americans did not answer these charges or counter with anti-Communist blasts, but American policy in Iran was based on information about the United States, not propaganda attacks on the Soviets.

The internal situation in Iran at the end of 1952 was difficult to gauge, for, although the national economy was in dire straits, when it came to individuals the oil crisis had hurt the workers in Abadan and the oil fields and the populace of Tehran much more than others. The Persian government at the end of 1951 had sold official automobiles and the rugs from government offices to raise money. Civil servants remained unpaid and, of course, most of the government projects and all industrial expansion had ceased. There was considerable unrest and grumbling among merchants who saw their sales decline while prices rose and the currency rates became a speculator's dream.

Most speculation by foreigners, however, centered on the question: Will Iran fall prey to the Communists? In spite of the deteriorating economic situation, with little prospect of a quick settlement of the oil controversy, there were a number of factors militating against a Tudeh *coup d'état*.

[9] Volume 27, no. 693 (Oct. 6, 1952), 536.

While the Tudeh might well have seized power in Tehran and Tabriz in 1952, the important position of the tribes and religious groups was a strong deterrent to precipitate action. The Communists, realizing that the loyalty of the tribesman was first to his chief and then to the government, sent agents into the villages and among the tribes to wean their followers away from the chiefs. Tudeh influence grew in the villages in 1952 but did not register much success with the tribesmen. Propaganda among the Kurds to establish an independent state usually had little effect because the Kurdish mountaineers were suspicious of the very word "state," no matter who controlled it, and their experience in 1946 had not been a happy one. They and the nomadic tribesmen to the south have always thought that they fared better when the central power was weak, and the idea of establishing a government which might well prove stronger than the present Tehran government was not to their liking. And any strong government would probably seek to settle the nomadic tribes on the land, which, while it might bring order and raise the standard of living of the nomad, would destroy his freedom. The tribes, well-armed, presented a major hurdle to Soviet ambitions, and it was the tribes rather than foreign interference which the Soviets feared, since by the Irano-Soviet Treaty of 1921 Russia had the right to move troops into Iran if foreigners prepared plots against the USSR on Iranian soil. So the Communists continued with slow but inexorable progress on their plan of exacerbating any troubles in the country and at the same time winning converts under cover until the day the country would fall like a ripe fruit into their hands. They looked far into the future by working in the schools and in the universities of Tehran, Tabriz, and Shiraz, for here as elsewhere in the Middle East they found their chief support. The intellectuals easily fell into Communist groups; but why was this true?

The intellectuals and professional people in Iran are extremely patriotic; they invariably support nationalist movements, but many feel frustrated because at present social and political reform is so slow. These intellectuals and middle-class urbanites feel that only a Communist revolution will accomplish the much-needed reforms, for they have an unrealistic concept of Soviet Russia as a state run by intellectuals and party leaders, not by peasants and workers. These Persians feel that they might well be in better economic and political positions under a Communist regime than they are now. Soviet agents play upon the naïveté of their Persian supporters, portraying the USSR as a land of milk and honey where everyone is happy, and urging the Persians to sabotage their government, which, they argue, in any case is only a tool for Western imperialism. At the same time it is not surprising to find rightist—one might say fascist— elements united with the Communists in seeking the overthrow of established order, and this, of course, is dangerous for democratic development.

This parallel attack from Communists and nationalists on so-called Western imperialism has much attraction, for the Persians do have a fear of the Western powers. It is difficult for Americans to understand this frame of mind, for surely the imperialism of the 19th century is gone and American intentions in Iran do not militate against the political sovereignty of the country. This is true, but the new imperialism is economic imperialism, and this looms large in the eyes of the Persians. The oil controversy is a case in point, and it is interesting to see how closely the United States is after all involved in it. As one economist well explained: "The core of the conflict is the tight control which the AIOC wishes to maintain over the sale and distribution of oil from Iran. The control operates in three ways. The first is through a fixed-price structure among all Middle East oil producers which allows for varying prices in the producing countries but provides for identical prices in the consuming countries. The Iranian government insists on having either a slice of the difference between the price of the oil delivered in Europe and its price at the Abadan refinery, or the freedom to cut prices on its own sales to new foreign customers. The second method is control by AIOC and the major oil companies of all tankers and storage and distributing facilities. Thirdly, AIOC and the other big oil companies have a monopoly over skilled oil men. Only in the United States can one hire independent drilling and refining crews, and these crews have been publicly discouraged by the United States government from bidding for work in Iran. This helps us to understand why Iran's ire, in the last instance, is directed against the well-entrenched, closely-knit international pattern of control over production, distribution, and sale of Middle East oil. Since both the British and the U.S. governments seem to defend this pattern, at least in their conduct of foreign affairs, they have become targets too."[10] It is no wonder, then, that the West has much to do to win the confidence of the peoples of underdeveloped areas.

Another point: Why do the intellectuals and professional people feel so frustrated and pessimistic about the future? It should be remembered that one can make a division of Iranian society into those who work with their hands and those who under no circumstances would indulge in manual labor. For the latter a livelihood is difficult to find outside the government bureaucracy, since the professions are as yet undeveloped and such organizations as insurance companies, advertising concerns, and a host of service enterprises are virtually unknown. Hence the graduate of the university or high school has little choice but government employment, and this for the most part is a dreary, unrewarding occupation, as portrayed by the short stories of Sadiq Hidayat.[11] The vast majority of the population—peasants and nomads —are a group apart, with little in common with the intellectuals in the towns. This, of course, is one of the main problems of the Orient today, and the absence of a strong middle class makes all of the countries of the Orient easy prey to Communist propaganda. There is at present in Iran no economic basis, indeed no stability, on which a middle class could develop. Consequently the students feel frustrated;

[10] P. G. Franck, "Economic Nationalism in the Middle East," *The Middle East Journal,* 6 (1952), 432-3.

[11] Cf. V. Monteil, *Sadeq Hedayat* (Tehran, 1952), 90 pp. (in French).

they see little hope for themselves in the future save the drudgery of a government job in the provinces. Without understanding Communist philosophy and aims they turn to it as a possible panacea for their own ills as well as the ills of the country. But one may ask why a middle class does not develop. In Iran there are other complicating factors besides age-old traditions and the lack of industrial development. Perhaps the most significant are the difficulty of organizing cooperation in business plus the lack of public spirit.

It has been stated that the Persians are an individualistic people, which is a source of weakness as well as strength, for it makes for difficulty in teamwork and cooperation in business or any other activity. Individual achievement and success are more highly considered and better rewarded perhaps than in the more socially conscious West, a West with at least a kind of social consciousness in business and industry as engendered by laws and circumstances. The number of business partnerships which have started well and then dissolved is legion in Iran, while public responsibility and feeling is still not widespread. Indeed, the example of Muhammad Nemazee, wealthy merchant of Shiraz, who constructed a hospital and a modern purification plant for the water of his native city, is unique. If much more of the youth of the country could be trained in technical subjects and in the trades, and if an educated and enlightened middle class of professional people, businessmen, and functionaries could develop with a consciousness of their responsibility to the entire population and their role in the improvement of living for all, then the future would look happier. But there is much to do, and the intellectuals are still groping, seeking quick solutions to their problems; or they are turning to religion, and the religious leaders, like the Communists, hope to gain by their discontent.

Rampant nationalism and strong religious sentiment have more in common than appears at a glance, for the religious leaders have seen their chance in supporting the nationalists on the oil question—the burning question of the day. The religious leaders seek to regain ground lost under Reza Shah and they have gained much popular support for their anti-British campaign and leadership in the nationalization movement. They feel they can control the Communists, but they too fear the West as a greater threat to their prerogatives as leaders, and anything which weakens the influence of the West in Iran is welcome to them; hence the possibility of developing a widespread xenophobia. The disillusionment of the intellectuals educated in Western fashion is exploited by the religious leaders, who decry what they term the arrogance of both Soviet Communism and Western materialism, both of which are blasphemous in placing man above God. To the intellectuals they say, "Learn the techniques of the West, but remember that Islam is still the one sure road to metaphysical truth. The pragmatic, materialist West can satisfy your body but only Islam can satisfy your soul." So argue some of the religious leaders in Iran today, and their admonishments do have an effect on many Persians.

The frustration and discontent of the intellectuals is reflected in the literature of the post-war period, which has developed with great strides after remaining comparatively dormant in the Reza Shah era. The growth of a free, if sometimes irresponsible, press bears witness to the temper of the intellectuals, but even more significant are the new styles and motifs in novels and essays. The writer in Iran plays a much more important and influential role than his American colleague. The modern Persian writer is more representative of his milieu and the beliefs of his fellowmen, and he is also a barometer of future trends. What are the trends in modern Persian literature which might give us an insight into the problems besetting the Persian writer and how he tries to solve them?

A good indication of the interests of the educated and the influences shaping their thinking can be obtained from a glance at the most significant foreign books translated into Persian after the war. The writings of the Czech Kafka and the surrealism of Sartre have been well received in Iran. Those, and others who are symptomatic of the Westerner's uncertainty in the great world of science created by him, interest the Persian intellectual who, to repeat, experiences doubts and suspicious about European civilization, which is so difficult to reconcile with his Iranian and Islamic traditions. Yet he realizes he must somehow reconcile them if he and his beloved country are to survive in the Atomic Age. So he wrestles with the suggestions of his religious people and with Western concepts, and the struggle frequently splits his loyalties and beliefs. And this suggests a question: "Why is it that the Persian, so rich in all the social gifts, so full of fun, possessed of such a happy and lively disposition, is so often, when he takes a pen in his hand and composes a story, a totally different kind of person, inclined to take a sombre view of life? It may be that the gaiety is on the surface, and beneath the gaiety, in the minds of most Persians, are a deep concern at the conditions in which so many of the people have to live; anxiety as to their country's future; too many memories of what Persia has endured in the past."[12]

The most interesting literary figures, men such as Hidayat, Jamalzadeh, and Chubak, turned to the common man, and in his own colloquial language wrote of his tribulations and suffering. The new poems and novels are filled with a cry against social injustice as well as against foreign exploitation of Iran. New currents in the literature are starting, as well as new ideas among the people, which may lead to social change; but if there will be change, surely it will be based on the heritage of the past of which the Persians are so proud. And if there come revolution and social change, one will yet speculate whether even they will really matter in the millennia of history which belong to the Orient. For, while Iran is still a land of uncertainty, so unpredictable in daily, monthly, or yearly happenings, yet in the long view one may wonder on the continuity, or repetition, and ultimate insignificance of the change itself. As Gertrude Bell says, "In the wilderness, between high walls, the secret, mysterious life of the East flows on—a life into which no European can pen-

[12] H. D. G. Law in *Life and Letters*, vol. 63 (London, Dec., 1949), 200.

etrate, whose standards, whose canons, are so different from his own that the whole existence they rule seems to him misty and unreal, incomprehensible, at any rate unfathomable; a life so monotonous, so unvaried from age to age that it does not present any feature marked enough to create an impression other than that of vague picturesqueness, of dullness inexpressible, of repose which has turned into lethargy, and tranquility carried beyond the point of virtue.

"And these gardens, also with their tall trees and peaceful tanks, are subject to the unexpected vicissitudes of Eastern fortune. The minister falls into disgrace, the rich merchant is ruined by the exactions of his sovereign; the stream is turned off, the water ceases to flow into the tanks and to leap in the fountains, the trees die, the flowers wither, the walls crumble into unheeded decay, and in a few years the tiny paradise has been swept forgotten from the face of the earth, and the conquering desert spreads its dust and ashes once more over it all."[13] So the old Iran; only the future will tell of the new.

[13] G. Bell, *Persian Pictures* (London, 1947), 31.

Bibliographical Note

INASMUCH as the history and background of Iran of necessity have been only briefly sketched, an ample bibliography would seem desirable. He who would read more about the Persians and their country will find that not only works of reference and detailed scholarship but also books of travel and fiction give an insight into the varied aspects of the land of the lion and the sun.

I. GENERAL WORKS AND BIBLIOGRAPHIES

There are many general works on Iran describing the land, commerce, and industry; perhaps the best factual survey is Donald N. Wilber, *Iran: Past and Present* (Princeton, 1948), 234 pp. A good cultural survey is *The Legacy of Persia*, ed. by A. J. Arberry (Oxford, 1952), 350 pp. Somewhat outdated but still useful is the book of Sir Arnold Wilson, *Persia* (New York, 1933), 400 pp., which is concerned with trade, government and the like. The same author also published *A Bibliography of Persia* (Oxford, 1930), 253 pp., but unfortunately it is only alphabetical and not annotated. The best bibliographical survey of Iran is L. P. Elwell-Sutton, *Guide to Iranian Area Study* (Washington, D. C., 1952), 235 pp. For linguistics and matters pertaining to Old Persian and Middle Persian the booklet by W. B. Henning, *Bibliography of Important Studies on Old Iranian Subjects* (Tehran, 1950), 53 pp., is to be recommended. The New York Public Library's *List of Books Relating to Persia* (New York, 1915), 151 pp., is helpful though now outdated; the *Selected and Annotated Bibliography of Books and Periodicals Dealing with the Near and Middle East*, edited by R. Ettinghausen (Washington, D. C., 1952), 111 pp., though covering the entire Near East, is classified and the contents of books described, with an author index. Cf. also the bibliography of H. F. Farman, *Iran* (Library of Congress, Washington, D. C., 1951), 100 pp. A discussion of post-war books on Iran was written by T. Cuyler Young for

The Middle East Journal, 4 (Washington, D. C., January 1950), 106-110, which, while limited, has the most detailed descriptions with critiques of books of any of the bibliographies.

2. GEOGRAPHY AND PEOPLES

Although the section on Iran is perhaps the weakest part of *The Middle East: A Physical, Social and Regional Geography* (New York, 1951), 514 pp. by W. B. Fisher, it is the only adequate regional geography we have. Maps, too, are scarce, although the chief of the geographical section of the Iranian army, brother of the late Prime Minister Razmara, has published some useful volumes including a guide to the streets of Tehran, a guide to other cities in Iran with street plans, and a geographical dictionary of place names, six volumes of which are printed. Maps of various sizes may be obtained from his office or from bookstores in Tehran, all, of course, in Persian. In English the *Survey of India* maps are perhaps the best available, while the National Geographic Society's map of Southwest Asia is adequate for ordinary purposes.

Anthropologists have recently discovered the Middle East and have published village and tribal studies about Palestine, Egypt, and elsewhere, but Iran has been relatively neglected. Carleton Coon in his *Caravan* (New York, 1951), 376 pp., discusses the Iranian tribes to a limited extent and gives a bibliography. W. O. Douglas in *Strange Lands and Friendly People* (New York, 1951), 336 pp., writes of the tribes but is not always reliable. One of the best general works about the everyday life and beliefs of Persians in the nineteenth century is *A Year Amongst the Persians* by E. G. Browne (Cambridge University Press, 1927), 594 pp. There are two books on Iran which may be called literary classics in English; the first is James Morier's *Hajji Baba of Ispahan*, first published in 1824, but with many editions, and the second is Gertrude Bell, *Persian Pictures* (London, 1947), 157 pp. The former is a novel about Persian life and character so informed and typical that many Persians, after it had been translated into Persian, could not believe it had been written by an Englishman. *Persian Pictures* is a book of delightful sketches of the old Iran.

The novel *Stripling* by B. Y. Mirza (New York, 1940) 319 pp., is an interesting account of a Persian youth, while the account of the Bakhtiyari trek from winter to summer quarters by Merian C. Cooper in *Grass* (New York, 1925), 362 pp., is a unique document. V. Minorsky has a number of articles on the tribes in the *Encyclopaedia of Islam* (Leiden, 1913-1938); cf. also his article on "The Tribes of Western Iran," *Journal of the Royal Anthropological Institute,* 75 (1945), 73-80. (A new edition of the *Encyclopaedia of Islam* is now underway.)

3. HISTORY

A short summary of Persian history may be found in E. D. Ross, *The Persians* (Oxford, 1931), 142 pp., while a more comprehensive account is given in two volumes by P. Sykes, *A History of Persia* (London, 1930). The pre-Achaemenid history of Iran is treated by George Cameron in his *History of Early Iran* (Chicago, 1936), 260 pp. The results of the Persepolis excavations by the Oriental Institute of the University of Chicago will be published in 1953 and succeeding years. For a preliminary report see Erich F. Schmidt, *The Treasury of Persepolis* (Chicago, 1939), 139 pp. A. T. Olmstead's *The History of the Persian Empire* (Chicago, 1948), 576 pp., is an impressive work on the political, cultural, and social history of the Achaemenids, though his conclusions on religion, as well as other subjects, are at times overly subjective. R. Ghirshman in his *L'Iran* (Paris, 1952), 330 pp., to be published also in the English Penguin series, gives an up-to-date cultural history of Iran from earliest times to the Arab conquest. Parallel to it is C. Huart and L. Delaporte, *L'Iran antique* (Paris, 1943), 516 pp. The cultural history of the Achaemenids is discussed in detail by M. Etécham, *L'Iran sous les Achéménides* (Fribourg, 1946), 195 pp.

For Parthian and Sassanian history the two basic works are N. Debevoise, *A Political History of Parthia* (Chicago, 1938), 303 pp., and A. Christensen, *L'Iran sous les Sassanides* (Copenhagen, 1944), 560 pp. The last word on Zoroaster was written by W. B. Henning, *Zoroaster* (Oxford, 1951), 51 pp. For a recent translation of the Gathas, the oldest part of the Avesta, see J. Duchesne-Guillemin, *The Gathas of Zoroaster* (London, 1952).

The Arab conquests and establishment of native Persian dynasties is discussed in detail by B. Spuler, *Iran in Früh-Islamischer Zeit* (Wiesbaden, 1952), 656 pp. On the minor dynasties see also Amir Hasan Siddiqi, *Caliphate and Kingship in Medieval Persia*

(Lahore, 1942), 184 pp. Persian art is covered in A. U. Pope's massive *Survey of Persian Art* in six volumes (Oxford, 1938-39). The Mongols in Iran are discussed in great detail by B. Spuler, *Die Mongolen in Iran 1220-1350* (Leipzig, 1939), 533 pp. Cf. also Guy Le Strange, *Mesopotamia and Persia under the Mongols in the Fourteenth Century A.D.* (London, 1903), 134 pp.

The age of the Safavids has been greatly neglected by Western scholars, and we have only one biography of Shah 'Abbas, which leaves much to be desired, by L. L. Bellan, *Chah 'Abbas I* (Paris, 1932), 297 pp. On Nadir Shah L. Lockhart has written an excellent account (London, 1938), 344 pp. The Qajar dynasty too has been neglected by European savants, but there is considerable material available on the revolution of 1906, perhaps the most extensive account being E. G. Browne, *The Persian Revolution of 1905-1909* (Cambridge U., 1910), 470 pp. The work by W. M. Shuster, *The Strangling of Persia* (New York, 1912), 423 pp., was a best seller in Iran after it was translated into Persian.

For German activities in Iran during the first World War cf. Christopher Sykes, *Wassmuss, the German Lawrence.* (New York, 1939), 271 pp. Sir Percy Sykes, who commanded the South Persia Rifles, describes the British position in Iran in the second volume of his history. The Persian side of relations with Britain and Russia after the War is told by Nasrollah S. Fatemi, *Diplomatic History of Persia, 1917-1923* (New York, 1952), 331 pp., while the British point of view appears in Hon. J. M. Balfour, *Recent Happenings in Persia* (London, 1922), 307 pp. The first Millspaugh mission in the 1920's is described by A. C. Millspaugh in *The American Task in Persia* (New York, 1925), while the story of his second mission, with an apology, is in his book *Americans in Persia* (Washington, D. C., 1946), 293 pp. Reza Shah's regime is portrayed by L. P. Elwell-Sutton, *Modern Iran* (London, 1941), 234 pp.; unfortunately we still have no good biography of the strong ruler.

The official story of the U.S. Army's Persian Gulf Command is in the book by T. H. Vail Motter, *The Persian Corridor and Aid to Russia* (Washington, D. C., U.S. Army; 1952), 545 pp. Soviet and Communist influences in Iran are studied by George Lenczowski in his *Russia and the West in Iran, 1918-1948* (Cornell U., 1949), 383 pp.

For recent events see Lenczowski's *The Middle East in World Affairs* (Cornell, 1952), 153-189, and L. V. Thomas and R. N.

Frye, *The United States and Turkey and Iran* (Harvard, 1952). Among recent "travel" literature Olive Suratgar, *I Sing in the Wilderness* (London, 1951), is to be recommended for its insight into present-day social affairs. Literature on oil can be found in abundance; cf. especially the documents, both from the Iranian side and from the AIOC, listed in *The Middle East Journal*, 6 (Spring, 1952), 267-8. For the current happenings the *New York Times* gives good coverage of Iran and is the best available source.

APPENDIX I

Statistics on Land and People[1]

Area: ca. 628,000 square miles.

Population: 18,771,538 (according to Persian newspapers on February 4, 1951).

The density of population is estimated at about 29 per square mile for the entire country. If the desert areas are excluded the estimate is about 43 per square mile for the country.

Vital Statistics: Infant mortality is estimated at 500 per thousand live births. The average rural life expectancy is estimated at 27 years.

Villages and Land: About 15-20 per cent of the people live in towns; 20-25 per cent are estimated to be semi-nomadic, while 65 per cent live in villages. There are over 40,000 villages according to one estimate. Eighty per cent of the population engages in agriculture. A 1949 survey of 1,300 villages showed that 60 per cent of the families were landless, 25 per cent owned less than 2½ acres, 10 per cent owned from 2½ to 7½ acres; while this same 95 per cent owned only 17 per cent of the total land. It is roughly estimated that at least half the claimed land is owned by large, often absentee, landowners numbering about 100,000. Religious endowments own about one fourth of the land; public and royal domain land constitutes less than 10 per cent of the total.

Cost of living and wholesale prices: (Index number 1939 = 100)

	Cost of Living	Wholesale Prices (Tehran)
1939	100	100
1940	111	113
1941	152	143

[1] The following figures have been taken from the journal *Middle Eastern Affairs*, 2 (June-July, 1951), 238-242, where sources are given. Some of the statistics are approximate.

	Cost of Living	*Wholesale Prices* (Tehran)
1942	269	252
1943	650	461
1944	757	500
1945	644	469
1946	577	453
1947	584	484
1948	640	526
1949	698	492
1950 (first half)	598	403

Livestock and Draught Animals: (in thousands)

	1946	*1948*
Cattle	2,500	2,100
Buffalo	11	..
Sheep	13,200	11,000
Goats	6,800	..
Horses	350	310
Donkeys	1,300	1,000
Mules	50	42

Imports and Exports: (in millions of *rials*)

	Imports	*Exports*
1949	7,481	18,960 (including oil)
1950	8,403	22,562 (including oil)

Persons employed and power available in principal industries—1948:

Industry	*Number of Employees*	*Horsepower*
Sugar refining	4,500	10,000
Textile	28,800	45,000
Chemical	4,600	3,000[2]
Match production	4,000[3]	..
Fishing	2,600	1,300
Mining	4,900	..
Electricity	600	19,000
Petroleum	62,000	85,000

[2] State-owned factories only.
[3] Eleven out of 26 establishments.

Production of Cereals: (in millions of quintals)

	1934-38	1945	1946	1947	1948	1949
Wheat	18.7	21.0	20.8	19.0	17.0	16.3
Barley	7.9	12.5	8.7	7.7	6.0	6.5
Maize	..	..	..	0.1	0.1	..
Rice	4.2	4.2	4.2	3.5	4.5	4.8
Total	30.8	37.7	33.7	30.3	27.6	..

Major Exports:

	1937-1938 (June 22-June 21)		1948-1949 (Year beginning March 21)	
Commodity	Pre-War Quantity (in tons)	Per Cent of Total Value of Exports	Post-War Quantity (in tons)	Per Cent of Total Value of Exports
Carpets	2,690	15.6	3,540	31.0
Fruits and nuts	52,410	13.3	48,030	24.1
Total		28.9		55.1

(Only the two major exports, by value, are given. Petroleum exports are excluded.)

Major Imports: (in thousands of metric tons, by groups of commodities)

	1948		1949	
	Quantity	Per Cent of Total Value	Quantity	Per Cent of Total Value
Cereals and milled products	4.8	0.3	25.0	2.4
Sugar and confectionery	94.8	11.9	87.6	7.7
Tea, coffee and cocoa	7.7	7.9	7.5	8.9
Wood, cork and articles thereof	1.7	0.1	2.5	0.3
Cotton, silk, rayon and wool	0.9	2.3	1.0	2.2
Cotton piece goods	4.6	10.2	7.1	19.8
Silk, rayon and woolen tissues	2.3	13.0	0.9	5.4
Petroleum and petroleum products	34.5	0.9	14.0	0.8

	1948 Quantity	*1948* Per Cent of Total Value	*1949* Quantity	*1949* Per Cent of Total Value
Chemical and pharmaceutical products	7.7	5.0	10.3	7.3
Rubber and rubber products	6.7	4.3	3.7	3.3
Paper and paper products	8.2	2.6	9.1	2.5
Common metals and metal manufactures	35.3	8.6	30.9	9.6
Machinery and appliances	4.9	6.1	5.9	7.6
Transport equipment	11.9	7.9	7.3	7.0
Other imports	39.2	18.9	34.4	15.2

(Imports by concessionaires have been excluded. "Concessionaires" refers mainly to the Anglo-Iranian Oil Company. The year ending is March 20.)

APPENDIX II

The Constitution of Iran[1]

THE constitution of Iran comprises the principal law of 1906, a supplement of 1907, a revision of 1925 (the accession to the throne of the Pahlevi dynasty), and an implementation of 1949 (realization of the articles concerning the establishment of the Senate and the dissolution of the parliament).

The principal law is composed of 51 articles divided into 5 chapters:

1. Organization of the Majlis (articles 1-14).
2. Rights, duties, and nature of the Majlis (15-31).
3. Submission of projects and bills to parliament (32-38).
4. Parliamentary initiative (39-42).
5. Institution of the Senate (43-51).

A law of October 22, 1911, fixed the number of deputies in the Majlis at 136, and their terms of office at two years. Article 7 states that "On the opening of the debates, at least two-thirds of the Members of the Assembly shall be present, and, when the vote is taken, at least three-quarters. A majority shall be obtained only when more than half of those present in the Assembly record their votes." The length of sessions of the Majlis is determined by the deputies and on the opening day the Shah addresses the Assembly. Article 12 guarantees parliamentary immunity to the deputies while article 13 states that the sessions of the Majlis must be public and newspapers have the right to print the contents of debates as long as they do not change them.

Article 16 declares that all laws must be submitted to the National Assembly for approval; and the Majlis, with Senate

---

[1] The constitution is reproduced in Helen Davis, *Constitutions, Electoral Laws, Treaties of States in the Near and Middle East* (Durham, N. C., 1947). I have used Ramesh C. Ghosh, *Constitutional Documents of the Major Islamic States* (Lahore, 1947).

approval, can abrogate or modify any existing law, according to article 17. All financial matters must be approved by the Majlis, while treaties, changes in frontiers, concessions, etc., must also be approved by that body. Article 28 states that any Minister who issues orders conflicting with one of the laws shall rescind the orders and be personally responsible to the Shah. The Majlis can demand the dismissal of a Minister who has violated a law, and it has access to the Shah through a committee of the Majlis. Ministers have the right to sit and speak in sessions of the National Assembly.

The mechanism whereby laws are made is explained in articles 32 and 33; the former states, "Any individual may submit in writing to the Petition Department of the Archives of the National Assembly a statement of his own case, or of any criticisms or complaints. If the matter concerns the Assembly itself, it will give him a satisfactory answer; but if it concerns one of the Ministries, it will refer it to that Ministry, which will enquire into the matter and return a sufficient answer." Article 33 continues, "New laws which are needed shall be drafted and revised in the Ministries which are respectively responsible, and shall then be laid before the Assembly by the responsible Ministers, or by the Prime Minister. After being approved by the Assembly, and ratified by the Royal Signature, they shall be duly put into force." Article 37 says, "If a measure introduced by any Minister is not accepted by the Assembly, it shall be returned supplemented by the observations of the Assembly; and the responsible Minister, after rejecting or accepting the criticisms of the Assembly, can propose the aforesaid measure a second time to the Assembly."

Whenever any measure is proposed on the part of one of the deputies it can only be discussed when at least fifteen members of the Assembly approve the discussion. In such cases the proposal should be forwarded in writing to the President of the Majlis, who will send it to a committee for study.

The Senate, which came into existence only in 1949 although its formation is approved by the constitution, consists of sixty members, thirty nominated by the Shah (half from Tehran and half from the provinces), and thirty elected by the people (half from Tehran and half from the provinces). All bills must be approved by the Senate as well as the Majlis, except financial measures, which are the sole responsibility of the Majlis. In case of a dispute between Senate and Majlis, article 48 provides for a third assembly elected by both Majlis and Senate to effect a compromise, but if that fails the Shah may dissolve the National Assembly and call for new elections.

The supplement of 1907 declared Shiite Islam the official religion of Iran and provided for the representation of at least five religious leaders in the Majlis who may collectively declare any legislation null and void if it conflicts with the principles of Islam. Further articles of the supplementary law gave a kind of Bill of Rights, providing Iranian citizens with equal rights before the law, protection from interference, illegal punishment, illegal seizure of property, and the like. Article 18 says, "The acquisition and study of all sciences, arts and crafts is free, save in the case of such as may be forbidden by ecclesiastical law." Freedom of press, association, and post is guaranteed except for cases which harm religion or state. Articles 26-34 divide the powers of the government into legislative, judicial, and executive, distinct and separate from one another. Articles 35-57 are concerned with the rights of the Throne, succession, minting in the name of the sovereign, etc.

According to article 58 no one can attain the rank of Minister unless he be a Muslim by religion, an Iranian by birth, and an Iranian subject. In the domain of justice article 71 states that "The Supreme Ministry of Justice and judicial tribunals are the places officially destined for the redress of public grievances, while judgment in all matters falling within the scope of ecclesiastical law is vested in just *mujtahids* possessing the necessary qualifications." According to article 80, "The presidents and members of the judicial tribunals shall be chosen in such manner as the laws of justice determine, and shall be appointed by Royal Decree."

In local government article 90 provided for the establishment of provincial councils to be set up in accordance with special regulations, and their chief function is to publish an account of the expenditure and income of every kind in the province.

The 107 articles of the supplementary law are perhaps more important than the original constitution itself, but together they are the fundamental law of the land.

APPENDIX III

The Tehran Declaration

THE President of the United States of America, the Premier of the U.S.S.R., and the Prime Minister of the United Kingdom, having consulted with each other and with the Prime Minister of Iran, desire to declare the mutual agreement of their three Governments regarding their relations with Iran.

The Governments of the United States of America, the U.S.S.R., and the United Kingdom recognize the assistance that Iran has given in the prosecution of the war against the common enemy, particularly by facilitating the transportation of supplies from overseas to the Soviet Union.

The three Governments realize that the War has caused special economic difficulties for Iran, and they are agreed that they will continue to make available to the Government of Iran such economic assistance as may be possible, having regard to the heavy demands made upon them by their world-wide military operations and to the world-wide shortage of transport, raw materials, and supplies for civilian consumption.

With respect to the post-War period, the Governments of the United States of America, the U.S.S.R., and the United Kingdom are in accord with the Government of Iran that any economic problem confronting Iran at the close of hostilities should receive full consideration, by conferences or international agencies held or created to deal with international economic matters.

The Governments of the United States of America, the U.S.S.R., and the United Kingdom are at one with the Government of Iran in their desire for the maintenance of the independence, sovereignty, and territorial integrity of Iran.

They count upon the participation of Iran, together with all other peace-loving nations in the establishment of international peace, security, and prosperity after the War in accord with the principles of the Atlantic Charter, to which all four Governments have continued to subscribe.

Index

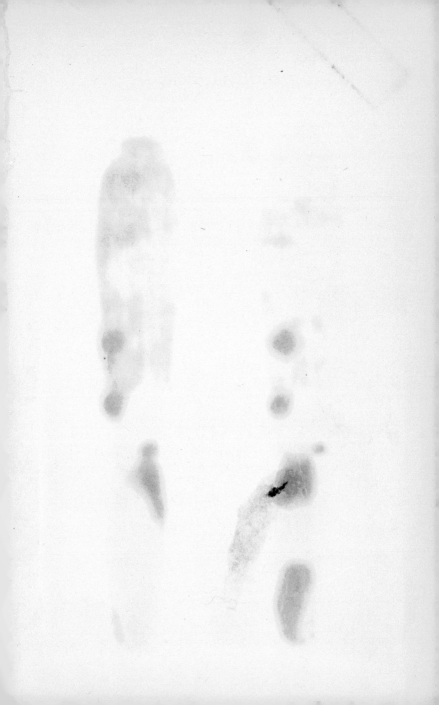

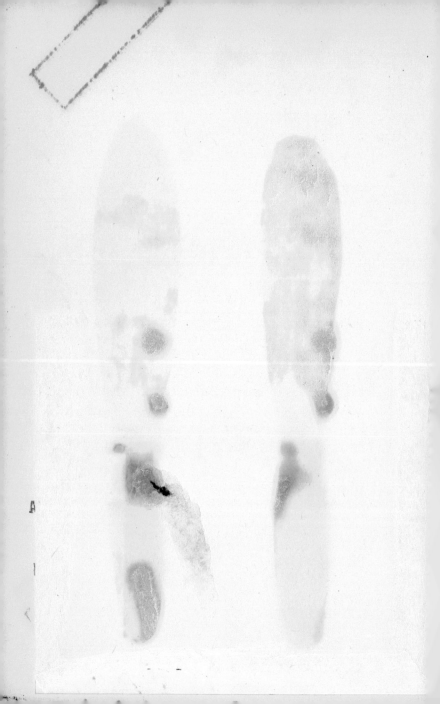